D1432808

AFRICAN DIPLOMACY

AFRICAN DIPLOMACY

Studies in the Determinants of Foreign Policy

EDITED BY

Vernon McKay

Published for the
School of Advanced International Studies
The Johns Hopkins University
by
FREDERICK A. PRAEGER, *Publishers*
New York · Washington · London

FREDERICK A. PRAEGER, PUBLISHERS
111 Fourth Avenue, New York, N.Y. 10003, U.S.A.
77–79 Charlotte Street, London W.1, England

Published in the United States of America in 1966
by Frederick A. Praeger, Inc., Publishers

Second printing, 1967

© 1966 by Frederick A. Praeger, Inc.

All rights reserved

Library of Congress Catalog Card Number: 66–13669

Printed in the United States of America

Foreword

In the fall of 1964, when Professor Vernon McKay suggested the desirability of convening a group of African specialists to explore the determining factors that shape the foreign policies of the new African states, I readily agreed. Some five years earlier, while still an official in the U.S. Department of State, I had had the privilege of making an intensive five-week study trip to the African continent. I came back from that trip fully convinced that the emergence of the new states of Africa on the world scene constituted one of the most important developments of this century. Just what role these new states will play as members of the international community and just what kind of an impact they will have on modern diplomacy are still open questions. It is obvious, however, that any serious study that can throw helpful light upon the determinants of African diplomacy should be welcomed not only by the academic world but also by practicing diplomats and by others interested in the evolving African scene.

Early in June, 1965, a conference of some forty specialists was convened at The Johns Hopkins School of Advanced International Studies for a three-day period. This volume is the result of those deliberations. On behalf of the School, I would like to express my deep appreciation to Professor McKay, who organized and conducted the conference and who edited this volume. I am also grateful to the six other contributors and to the participants generally whose collective expertise was so very helpful in producing the pages that follow.

One of Ghana's leading figures once remarked that "what we

want from the United States is sympathy for our aspirations and understanding for our mistakes." I am confident that this little volume will make a valuable contribution to that end.

Francis O. Wilcox, Dean
School of Advanced International Studies
The Johns Hopkins University
Washington, D.C.

The Contributors

L. Gray Cowan is Professor of Government and Director of the Institute of African Studies, The School of International Affairs, Columbia University. He is the author of *Local Government in West Africa* (1958) and *Dilemmas of African Independence* (1964) and co-editor of *Education and Nation-Building in Africa* (1965).

William J. Foltz, Assistant Professor of Political Science at Yale University, is the author of *From French West Africa to the Mali Federation* (1965).

Andrew M. Kamarck is Lecturer on African Affairs at the School of Advanced International Studies, The Johns Hopkins University, Washington, D.C., and Director of the Economics Department, International Bank for Reconstruction and Development. A contributor to *The Economic Development of Uganda* (1962), *The United States and Africa* (1963), *Economic Transition in Africa* (1964), *The African World* (1965), and *Africa: A Handbook to the Continent* (rev. ed., 1966), he is the author of a forthcoming volume, *The Economics of African Development*.

Robert A. Lystad is Professor of African Studies at the School of Advanced International Studies, The Johns Hopkins University. He has done field work in Ghana and the Ivory Coast and is a member of the Permanent Council of the International Congress of Africanists. He is the author of *The Ashanti: A Proud People* and editor of *The African World: A Survey of Social Research* (1965).

Vernon McKay, Professor of African Studies and Director of the Program of African Studies at the School of Advanced International Studies of The Johns Hopkins University, is the author of *Africa in World Politics* (1963) and co-author of *Apartheid and United Nations Collective Measures* (1965). President of the African Studies Association in 1961–62, he is also chairman of the U.S. Department of State's Advisory Council on African Affairs.

C. T. Thorne, Jr., is a research specialist in African affairs, with a particular interest in Africa's international relations.

I. WILLIAM ZARTMAN, who gained firsthand knowledge of North African life during two years of work and research in Morocco, was formerly Associate Professor of International Studies at the University of South Carolina and is presently Professor of Government and International Relations at New York University. He is the author of *Government and Politics in Northern Africa* (1963), *Destiny of a Dynasty* (1964), *Morocco: Problems of New Power* (1964), and *International Relations in the New Africa* (1966).

Contents

Introduction

In analyzing the factors that shape the foreign relations and foreign policies of African states, the authors of this volume pose many questions. If power is a prerequisite for a foreign policy, can weak African states really have enough of a foreign policy to merit analysis? Are African states still too new to have discovered and developed the national interests on which foreign policies are based? How practicable is it to separate African foreign policies from domestic policies for purposes of analysis at this early stage in their history? To what extent is it valid to classify the foreign policies of African states into radical, moderate, and conservative, or other categories? Although the passing of time will provide more data and make possible a more balanced perspective on such questions, it is nonetheless interesting and useful to undertake a comparative study of African diplomacy as it appears today.

Four possibilities of organizing the subject were considered. One alternative was a series of studies of the foreign policies of individual African states. The second was a series of case studies of particular issues that have had major effects on African diplomacy, such as the Congo crisis and apartheid in South Africa. The third was a comparative study along the lines finally adopted, but more conventional in organization, dividing the determinants of African diplomacy into geographical, historical, and biographical (personality) factors.

It seemed more fruitful, however, to attempt a comparative study in which authors from different academic disciplines—anthropology, economics, history, and political science—would

concentrate on the economic, cultural, military, and political determinants of African diplomacy. Each author was asked to be
multidisciplinary in approach in the sense of weaving the relevant
geographical, historical, and other factors into his own topic. To
minimize overlapping treatment of the subject, the authors circulated preliminary outlines of their papers to each other. The
complete papers were then circulated in advance to forty participants who met to discuss them at a symposium at the School of
Advanced International Studies of The Johns Hopkins University
on June 2–4, 1965.

My opening chapter on international conflict patterns in Africa
is designed as an introduction to the types of foreign-policy problems that challenge the ingenuity of African leaders. I. William
Zartman's stimulating analysis of national interest and ideology
demonstrates the practical functions of ideology in African foreign policies. Andrew M. Kamarck weighs both the internal and
external economic forces at work in Africa and the economic
structures of the new states as determinants of their foreign policies. African arms and armies are described by William J. Foltz,
who analyzes the extent to which military factors influence the
makers of foreign policy. The cultural and psychological processes
that affect Africa's rapidly changing societies are probed by anthropologist Robert A. Lystad in an assessment of their significance
for foreign policy. Political determinants inside Africa are considered by L. Gray Cowan, who studies both the role of foreign
policy in nation-building within each state, and the foreign relations of African states with each other. The impact of pressures
from the great powers is elaborated with clarity and insight by
C. T. Thorne, Jr. In a concluding chapter, I attempt to synthesize
the highlights of the symposium discussion in order to pinpoint
the African foreign-policy problems on which further research
is needed.

The authors wish to express their gratitude to the symposium
participants for their many valuable criticisms and suggestions.
Some of their comments were incorporated by the authors when
revising their chapters, and others are presented in summary form
in the final chapter of the book. In addition to the seven authors,
the participants were: Douglas G. Anglin, Carleton University,

Canada; Margaret Bates, Smith College; William O. Brown, Boston University; Gwendolen M. Carter, Northwestern University; Ronald Cohen, Northwestern University; Walter W. Deshler, University of Maryland; Wilton S. Dillon, National Academy of Sciences; Neville Dyson-Hudson, The Johns Hopkins University; J. Wayne Fredericks, U.S. Department of State; Peter Garlick, Howard University; Harvey Glickman, Haverford College; John Karefa-Smart, Columbia University; Helen Kitchen, Editor, *Africa Report;* Mbiyu Koinange, Minister of Education, Kenya; William H. Lewis, School of Advanced International Studies; John A. Marcum, Lincoln University; Karl Mathiasen, The Brookings Institution; Ruth Schachter Morgenthau, Brandeis University; Benjamin Nimer, The George Washington University; Claude S. Phillips, Jr., Western Michigan University; Darrell Randall, The American University; Arnold Rivkin, International Bank for Reconstruction and Development (IBRD); Carl G. Rosberg, University of California, Berkeley; Leslie I. Rubin, Howard University; Nathan Shamuyarira, Princeton University; Hugh H. Smythe, Brooklyn College; Albert Tevoedjre, Harvard University; Cecil H. Thompson, IBRD; Francis O. Wilcox, School of Advanced International Studies; W. Howard Wriggins, Washington Center of Foreign Policy Research, School of Advanced International Studies; M. Crawford Young, University of Wisconsin.

I wish to add my personal appreciation to those graduate students in the Program of African Studies at the School of Advanced International Studies who served as *rapporteurs* for the discussion of the symposium papers. The concept of the book, in fact, evolved originally out of my discussions with graduate students in a weekly seminar, The Foreign Policies of African States, which I first conducted in 1959.

VERNON McKAY

I

International Conflict Patterns

VERNON McKAY

"What would you expect to find, when the muzzle that has silenced the voices of black men is removed? That they would thunder your praise?" In these opening lines of his *Black Orpheus*, Jean-Paul Sartre illuminates a cardinal fact about the voices of Africa today. Radicalism is inherent in the new Africa. The African eagle, long kept on the ground and tamed as a chicken, has at last stretched forth its wings to fly.[1]

The American planes that dropped Belgian paratroopers into the heart of Africa to rescue white hostages touched upon the raw nerve of African radicalism. In the heated debate in the U.N. Security Council in December, 1964, according to Ambassador Adlai Stevenson, the United States was accused

of "wanton aggression", of "premeditated aggression", of plotting a humanitarian mission as a "pretext" for military intervention, of a "nefarious action" designed "to exterminate the black inhabitants", of "inhumanitarianism", of a "wanton and deliberate massacre of Congolese people", of "a murderous operation", of a "premeditated and cold-blooded act", of "not being truly concerned with the lives of the hostages", of a "crude subterfuge", of "massive cannibalism", of having killed Lumumba "with cynicism and premeditation", of genocide against an entire people, of being caught "red-handed", of

[1] The imagery of the eagle is adapted from a parable made popular by an earlier Gold Coast educator, J. E. K. Aggrey.

using the United Nations as a "Trojan horse", of a racist attack to kill thousands of "blacks", an operation which, in the words of one of the speakers, proved to him that a "white, if his name is Carlson, or if he is an American, a Belgian or an Englishman, is worth thousands upon thousands of blacks."[2]

Although accustomed to such torrents of abuse from Communist countries, many Americans were startled and angered to hear it from Africans, even though the more extreme attacks came from the diplomats of only a small number of militant African states.

Africans are even more vehement in their hostility toward the apartheid policy of the government of South Africa. Although divided over what to do about the Congo crisis, Africans are unanimous in their undying antagonism toward a system of white domination which discriminates against Africans because of their race. African diplomats have been extremely aggressive and highly inventive in a skillful effort to bring pressure on the United States and the United Kingdom, in particular to support U.N. economic sanctions against South Africa. Lacking the power to induce a change in South African policy themselves, they are trying to get others to do it for them. Thus far frustrated in their efforts, they are now using one weapon they do have, their votes in the U.N. and the Specialized Agencies, in a campaign to expel South Africa from some of these organs. For example, in Geneva on May 20, 1965, they won the necessary two-thirds majority on a proposal for a constitutional amendment that would enable the World Health Organization to suspend or exclude any member nation it considers guilty of racial discrimination. The vote was 65 to 29 with 10 abstentions. On an earlier occasion, on October 11, 1961, a Liberian representative startled Western delegates by proposing to expunge from U.N. records a speech by South African Foreign Minister Eric Louw in the General Assembly. After being revised into "a vote of censure against the Government of South Africa or its representative for a statement here today which was offensive, fictitious, and erroneous," the motion was adopted by 67 to 1 with 20 abstentions.

[2] For complete text, see "Statement by Ambassador Adlai E. Stevenson, United States Representative to the United Nations, in the Security Council on the Congo Question," U.S. Mission to the United Nations, Press Release No. 4479, December 14, 1964.

Can such tactics be called new techniques of a distinctively "African diplomacy," or are they only the techniques of new diplomats? Is the "African personality" expressing itself in a new diplomacy? Or is there nothing new about such tactics except the environment in which they are used?

The environment in which African diplomacy operates is certainly the important factor. It is my purpose to highlight the general nature of that environment, while the following chapters will analyze in depth the economic, cultural, military, and political factors or determinants that shape the foreign relations and the foreign policies of African states. The behavior of African diplomats is obviously a highly subjective matter of less importance. In any case, the style of individual African leaders and diplomats varies so much that it is doubtful if one can interpret "African diplomacy" to mean anything more than the diplomacy conducted by Africans. It should be recognized, however, that African leaders do have an élan and a sense of mission in their approach to international relations, a genuine belief that they are speaking for the underprivileged of the world, which was a strong motif in Indian diplomacy in the 1950's.

African diplomacy operates in a milieu of internal stress and strain, compounded by a multitude of external pressures. It is clear that the quick rise of African states is one of the major revolutions of the twentieth century, but our understanding of its meaning and ramifications is beclouded by the fact that it is not yet complete. Not only have Africans not yet freed their compatriots in the white redoubt in southern Africa, but in northern and middle Africa the political revolution that brought African leaders to power has understandably failed to satisfy the economic and social needs of the people.

In international relations, African states, which in 1951 numbered only four, have jumped to nearly forty with still more to come—a sharp contrast with the state systems of Europe, Asia, and the Americas, each of which has only about twenty members. Aside from the natural confusion and uncertainties precipitated by the sudden appearance of so many inexperienced states at a peak in the Cold War, two key facts stand out. One is the existence of many pockets of instability, and the other is the related involvement of the great powers in Africa. The danger lies in the combination of the two. As the world learned in 1960 in the Congo, every pocket of instability is a potential temptation for great power intervention. And every intervention by a great power raises at least some risk of leading to a direct confrontation between the two nuclear superpowers. It is this struggle between Soviet and Western powers that gives African states without strong arms and armies the kind of influence that enables them to conduct active foreign policies.

International conflict patterns in Africa are difficult to classify precisely, because they are new and constantly changing. In general, however, they may be divided into four types: (1) conflicts inside each state, (2) conflicts among or between African states, (3) conflicts among or between great powers over Africa, and (4) conflicts among or between African states and the great powers. Although the first type is basically internal rather than international, it must be included because of its interaction with the other three types.

Conflicts Inside Africa

A basic conflict pattern in Africa today is the growth of tension resulting from instabilities within individual states. These domestic struggles are closely related to foreign policy. Each author in this volume has his own way of explaining and classifying them. To me, they seem to have four general, overlapping origins. The first is the competition between the ruling group and the "outs." It is largely a struggle of elites for personal power, irrespective of ethnic or specific interest conflicts. Second is the conflict between the ruling group and specific interest group such as labor, youth, farmers, the church, and the military. Third is the conflict between ethnic groups or between a ruling ethnic group and those ruled. And finally, in certain states there are conflicts of a racial type, e.g., between whites and Africans, or between Indians and Africans.

African tensions are superficially reflected in many recent riots, plots, mutinies, *coups d'état*, and assassinations. President Kwame Nkrumah of Ghana was the target of at least five assassination attempts. Nigeria's stability was threatened by a cabal by leading politicians of the Western Region's Action Group in October, 1962, a startling event that contributed to the uneasy atmosphere, culminating in the electoral crisis of January, 1965.

Leaders of the French-speaking states have also been under attack. President Sylvanus Olympio of Togo, target of three plots, was assassinated in January, 1963, and his successor Nicolas Grunitzky has confronted new conspiracies. Two unsuccessful intrigues inspired by tribal and ideological differences have been directed against the regime of President Félix Houphouet-Boigny of the Ivory Coast. In Senegal, Prime Minister Mamadou Dia waged an unsuccessful revolt against President Léopold Senghor in December, 1962, as a consequence of which Dia was sentenced to life imprisonment. Two conspiracies have been reported against the government of President Sékou Touré in Guinea; and President Hamani Diori in Niger faces a continuing source of instability in the activities of the outlawed Sawaba Party, which has been using Ghana and Dahomey as sanctuaries. The regime of President François Tombalbaye of Chad has confronted several emergencies of ethnic and other origins.

In addition to the Togo coup that resulted in Olympio's death, other successful uprisings in French-speaking Africa include the overthrow of President Fulbert Youlou in Congo (Brazzaville) in August, 1963, and the toppling of President Hubert Maga by Colonel Christophe Soglo and an 800-man army in Dahomey in September, 1963. Those successes may have encouraged army figures in Gabon to attempt a similar overthrow of President Léon M'Ba in March, 1964, but the French Army acted quickly under its defense accords to restore the pro-French regime.

In northern Africa and the Horn, there have been several *coups d'état* in Egypt and the Sudan, as well as riots and fighting in Libya. President Ahmed Ben Bella of Algeria, who upset Benyoussef Ben Khedda, was overthrown by General Houari Boumedienne, and the Tunisian and Moroccan heads of state have both been intended victims of coups. In December, 1960, the world was surprised by an abortive uprising against the time-tested Emperor Haile Selassie of Ethiopia. The ethnic split between Arabs in the northern Sudan and Negroid peoples in the South remained the principal issue in Sudanese politics.

In East and Central Africa, immediately after the Sultan of Zanzibar was deposed in January, 1964, mutinies broke out in Tanganyika, Kenya, and Uganda; they were put down with the help of British troops. The Bahutu in Rwanda killed thousands of Watutsi. In June, the surprising return to the Congo (Leopoldville) of Moise Tshombe, as Prime Minister, who often had been accused of complicity in the murder of Patrice Lumumba, was followed by rebel massacres of both blacks and whites and by new forms of foreign intervention. The Tshombe regime lasted less than eighteen months, however, falling on November 25, 1965. Within the next ninety days, the heads of five other African states —the Central African Republic, Dahomey, Upper Volta, Nigeria, and Ghana—also were ousted by military leaders.

African heads of state naturally are worried about these internal instabilities. For perspective, however, one may recall that, though independent for a century and a half, Latin American states still have enough mutinies, *coups d'état*, and revolutions to compete with Africa's record. Moreover, most of the African leaders who won independence for their countries are still in power; in fact, some who seemed most vulnerable have surprised observers by their staying power.

Africa's troubles are nonetheless symbolic of a basic instability that could breed greater conflict. Political opposition groups, labor groups, youth groups, and others on the radical left will seek to exploit failures to meet rising expectations by calling for drastic social change to complete the African revolution. Out-of-power opportunists on the right may well seek to exploit in certain areas a natural "resistance to change," the widespread and varied ethnic revivalism that expresses itself in numerous ways but is usually given the ambiguous label of "tribalism."

CONFLICTS AMONG AFRICAN STATES

Conflicts between individual African states and among rival groups of states are analyzed from various points of view by several of our authors. In the main, these rivalries are personal, ideological, or territorial in character. Personal rivalries of certain African leaders are neither ideological nor territorial but rather are competitions for influence, such as the rivalry of President

Senghor of Senegal and President Houphouet-Boigny of the Ivory Coast within French-speaking Africa and the friction between Presidents Nasser of the U.A.R. and Nkrumah of Ghana over Nasser's efforts to expand his influence south of the Sahara.

Ideological conflicts revolve around the militant tactics employed mainly by Ghana, Guinea, Mali, Algeria, and the U.A.R. to press for quicker freedom, unity, and development throughout Africa.

Territorial disputes include border delimitation controversies such as the Algerian-Moroccan dispute; irredentist movements of the Somali type; friction between Ghana and Togo over the border that divides the Ewe people; and competition for economic resources such as grazing lands on the Somali-Ethiopian border and minerals in Algeria and Mauritania.

Since many observers have prophesied the coming of a new conflict pattern of border wars and irredentist movements in Africa, it is worth pointing out that, thus far, the evidence does not confirm the prophecy. In the European state system from which we draw most of our theories about international relations, border conflicts and irredentist movements were a major determinant of national attitudes toward alliances and armaments. The unification of Germany and the subsequent settlement of the Franco-German border in 1871 contributed to the pattern of alliances and the armaments race that led to World War I.

Thus far, however, relatively few efforts have been made to change the arbitrary political boundaries established by those who colonized Africa. If Africans began to reshape borders according to ethnic, linguistic, religious, and cultural criteria, Africa could have not forty countries but hundreds of tribal states. Africa's first-generation nationalist leaders are fully aware of the potential Pandora's box that might result from too much tribal self-determination. Fear of parochial chaos has combined with what Julius Nyerere has called Africa's "sense of unity." Out of the Summit Conference at Addis Ababa that established the Organization of African Unity (OAU) in May, 1963, came the "spirit of Addis," which proclaimed mutual respect for the territorial integrity of African states and the desire for peaceful settlement of disputes. The force of this spirit was exhibited in the successful negotiation of cease-fires in the border crises between Algeria and Morocco, and between Somalia and Ethiopia, under pressure from organs of the OAU. Unfortunately, the continuing turmoil over the Congo crisis is undermining this sense of unity.

Since most of Africa's leaders have not yet consolidated their internal positions, in most cases they do not constitute a direct threat to each other; they can increase their power without its being at the expense of their neighbors. This acceptance of the inherited order, at least as a starting point, is reflected in the fact that Africa has not developed hostile military alliances and arms races or the kind of balance of power based on them. Rather, a "confederal," regional approach to security, not unlike that of Latin America, has combined with the continuing presence of France and Britain, and with U.S. support for the U.N., to give Africa some degree of order.

The chief test of the spirit of Addis comes from Somalia, which claims French Somaliland and about one-fifth of the national territory of both Kenya and Ethiopia. In the councils of the OAU, Somalia contends that there can be no talk of unity until Africa's "misdrawn" boundaries are revised. In November, 1963, the news was revealed that Somalia had rejected an American-West German-Italian military aid package in favor of a much larger Soviet offer, totaling about $30 million. The Russians and the Somalis claimed that the arms provided would supply an "internal security" force of 20,000, but the deal naturally aroused further tension in the area. The fundamentally revisionist Somalia seems likely to continue to search, wherever it can, for arms and support. Moreover, the Somali imbroglio has produced the first African case of two states' allying themselves against a third; on July 13, 1963, Kenya and Ethiopia reportedly signed a mutual defense and cooperation agreement, the terms of which have not been made public. Since Kenya and Ethiopia have close ties with Britain and the United States, and Britain has interests in the Gulf of Aden, while Somalia has signed recent aid agreements with Russia and China, there are possibilities of dangerous conflict in the area. The undecided factor is the degree to which Somalia is willing to isolate itself from Pan-African trends by threatening the basic rules of the game.

There are numerous examples of other states that make territorial claims against each other even though they lack ethnic, religious, and linguistic homogeneity. On the basis of claims of historic suzerainty in the area, Moroccan irredentism covers not only parts of Algeria but a section of Mali and all of Mauritania. Upper Volta has been subjected to pressure from both Mali and Ghana. Togo and Ghana have a continuing border dispute involving ethnic claims. Attempts by Dahomey and Niger to settle a dispute over possession of the five-mile-long Lete Island in the Niger River led to a near-rupture in their relations. Other examples could also be cited.

As far as irredentist dangers are concerned, however, Africa is perhaps fortunate in having few other states of the Somali type which have a common indigenous language, religion, and culture. For there is little reason to suppose that nationalism of this type will produce foreign policies basically different from those it has produced in Europe or elsewhere.

Perhaps the most disturbing innovation among African states is a new conflict pattern of interstate subversion or hidden intervention. Later in this chapter, I shall discuss the role of the OAU's Liberation Committee in encouraging and subsidizing subversive activities in the white redoubt in Southern Africa. Here the emphasis is on the efforts of certain independent African states to undermine each other. Interstate subversion to aid the rebels in the Congo has received the most publicity, but there are numerous other examples.

African anxieties over such subversion are formally expressed in the OAU Charter's proclamation of "Unreserved condemnation . . . of political assassination as well as of subversive activities on the part of neighbouring States or any other States" (Article III). At the time, the inclusion of this principle in the Charter was interpreted as a victory of the moderates over the radicals. The actual extent of subversion is difficult to assess, but its widespread potential is made possible by the existence of large numbers of political refugees in Africa. Interstate subversion requires cooperation between domestic opposition groups and foreign agents. Since the one-party states of Africa suppress their political opponents, Africa has more than its share of political leaders who have fled their countries to escape prison. The major refugee problem is that of the Watutsi who fled into neighboring countries from Rwanda and formed the Inyenzi, an exile movement supported by 160,000 refugees. Other important groups of refugees are the 40,000 who fled from southern Sudan; the 250,000 from Angola who crossed the border into the Congo; the 8,000 to 10,-000 refugees from Mozambique in Tanzania; the 30,000 refugees from Portuguese Guinea; the many hundreds from South Africa, South West Africa, and Rhodesia; and the 10,000 Congolese who fled from the rebels who rose in May, 1964.

The presence of so many refugees within their borders poses grave problems for African governments, and often it is difficult to determine the extent to which the aid received by these refugee-rebels is humanitarian or political. Some of the new governments do not have the staffs needed to control the refugee traffic. In certain instances, governments extend sanctuary to political refugees; in others, they facilitate political conspiracies against their neighbors; but in a few cases, they actually allow their territory to be used as a base for rebel military operations across the border.

In the Sudan and Rwanda, the roots of subversion are to a large extent ethnic. In Southern Africa, they lie in the struggle of Africans for liberation from white racial domination. In North and West Africa, subversive activities, though partly ethnic, have more of an ideological orientation. Militant states such as Algeria, the U.A.R., Ghana, and Guinea, which seek to convert other states to their views, find subversion a useful tool for achieving certain foreign-policy objectives. Overt military aggression is not only too expensive but would openly violate the Addis principle of mutual respect for territorial integrity. Subversion is not only easier to conceal but can be denied.

Some French-speaking states especially have been targets of interstate subversion. Opposition groups from Togo, Upper Volta, Niger, and Cameroon are in exile in Guinea and Ghana. Their activities prompted a major resolution at the Monrovia Conference of May 8–12, 1961, which urged "that all African and Malagasy States shall refrain from encouraging directly or indirectly, dissident groups or individuals of other States in subversive activities by permitting their own States to be used as bases from which such dissidents may operate, or by financing dissidents in other countries." In the Addis spirit of unity, Ghana announced a new policy on political asylum in June, 1963, declaring in particular that refugees would not be given material assistance for subversion or be permitted to "do anything whatsoever against the government and the institutions of their country." By the end of 1964, however, intra-African relations had again deteriorated, especially over the Congo rebellion, and Ghana was under renewed charges of subversion. Ghana and Dahomey are providing asylum for Djibo Bakary's Sawaba Party, exiled from Niger since 1959. In September and October, 1964, the government of Niger crushed a Sawaba rebellion, and in April, 1965, rebels allegedly trained in Communist China unsuccessfully tried to assassinate President Diori. Rebel leader Bakary is based in Accra, and authorities in Niger naturally denounce Ghana for encouraging subversion.

When the Organization Commune Africaine et Malgache (OCAM) was formed by all of France's former colonies in Black Africa except Guinea and Mali, its final communiqué of February, 1965, declared that member states "energetically condemn the action of certain states, notably Ghana, which harbor agents of subversion and organize training camps on their national territory."

The refugee problem and the related issue of rebel subversive activities are also significant because of the response they stimulate in the outside world. The reaction is well illustrated in a statement made to the U.S. Senate Judiciary Committee's Subcommittee on Refugees and Escapees on January 21, 1965, by G. Mennen Williams, Assistant Secretary of State for African Affairs. Pointing out the efforts of Moscow and Peking to penetrate refugee groups, Williams described U.S. support for various programs of assistance to African refugees, including a scholarship program for students from Southern Africa, about 200 of whom were then studying in the United States. Although Williams emphasized the humanitarian reasons for the program, its political implications were not overlooked by the governments of Portugal and South Africa. Those governments are also annoyed by the activities of outside private organizations such as the African-American Institute, which operates two secondary training schools, one in Tanzania and one in Zambia, each designed for 300 students, about 75 per cent of whom are refugees.

CONFLICTS AMONG THE GREAT POWERS OVER AFRICA

The third major conflict pattern is the rivalry among the great powers over Africa—a struggle that involves not only the United States, the Soviet Union, and Communist China, but the NATO powers as well. Although Africans often tell the West to "keep the Cold War out of Africa," some of them regard it as a blessing in disguise because it improves their prospects for getting aid from both sides. Moreover, it gives Africans a status and importance in international meetings well beyond their physical power because it enhances their bargaining position in their attempt to win support from the great powers for U.N. resolutions, offices, and Council and Commission memberships they seek. The former Algerian leader Ferhat Abbas wrote in his book *La Nuit coloniale,* "Without the existence and power of the socialist world, we would still be at the stage of colonialist literature and wordy promises of Woodrow Wilson."

Considerable speculation has recently been devoted to the possibility of a Soviet-American *détente* and its effects on Africa. For example, would a *détente* lead to a reduction of armaments and thereby free more funds for economic aid to Africa? Or would it only weaken the U.S. Administration in its annual battle with Congress for appropriation of foreign aid? On balance, it seems unlikely that a Soviet-American *détente* would change the underlying goals of the United States and the U.S.S.R. in Africa. The Soviet Union would still support the "liberation" of Africa, while the United States would still attempt to prevent the expansion of Communism. Possibly neither would consider it safe to lower its level of aid to Africa.

It is possible, however, that a thaw in the Cold War might make certain African leaders somewhat less ideologically oriented, at least on certain issues. In their rationale for nonalignment, African leaders frequently stress their positive role as a "third force" for international peace and stability. To the extent that hostility between the first and second forces diminishes, the rationale for an ideological third force is partially undermined.

It should be emphasized, however, that the Cold War is not the key issue to Africans. They remain preoccupied with the domestic imperatives of nation-building and economic development, while striving simultaneously to build African unity and to free the rest of Africa from white supremacy and foreign rule.

The possibility of a thaw in the Cold War has been reduced by the Sino-Soviet rift and the mounting Chinese penetration of Africa, as well as by U.S. military actions in Viet-Nam and the Dominican Republic. Whatever the United States and the U.S.S.R. do, Peking is now engaged in an interventionist policy apparently designed to develop, in the long run, a new revolutionary International among the poor peoples of Asia, Africa, and Latin America. If Peking's plan were to succeed, in coming decades the struggle between Communism and democracy might recede into the background as a new conflict develops between the "haves" and the "have-nots." Such a prospect recalls the fanciful suggestion, in 1958, of a French writer, Eugène Guernier, that perhaps Russia will even join the West when China takes Siberia as its first colony! In any event, this new brand of revisionism is forcing both the Soviet Union and the United States to react to a new threat in Africa. It seems likely to accelerate both Soviet and Western aid to the countries of middle Africa and to give a new impetus to Soviet subversive activities in Southern Africa.

Peking's efforts in Africa date back at least to the 1955 Bandung Conference, where numerous contacts with African leaders were made. Official Chinese delegations began to visit Black Africa in 1958, and Chinese embassies were opened in Khartoum in 1958, Conakry in 1959, Accra in 1960, and Mogadishu in 1961. Meanwhile, larger numbers of visiting delegations and African students were traveling between Africa and Peking. By 1963, Peking's struggle for ideological supremacy over Moscow was in full bloom in Africa. A declaration on November 30, by the Chinese Committee for Afro-Asian Solidarity proclaimed that the time to act had come, particularly in Angola, Mozambique, Portuguese Guinea, French Somaliland, Bechuanaland, South West Africa, and South Africa. Chinese attacks on the Soviet policy of coexistence were so bitter at the meeting of the Afro-Asian Peoples Solidarity Organization in Algiers in March, 1964, that the Sino-Soviet rift threatened to break up the organization. Africa's new priority in Chinese foreign policy reached a peak early in 1964, when Premier Chou En-lai and a staff of about sixty made a widely publicized seven-week visit to ten African countries.

By the end of 1964, Peking had made commitments of approximately $364 million in economic and military aid, including grants and credits to Algeria, the Central African Republic, Congo (Brazzaville), Congo (Leopoldville), Ghana, Guinea, Kenya, Mali, Somalia, Tanzania, and the U.A.R., as well as small subsidies to politicians and rebel leaders in several Southern African and other territories. Peking had seventeen diplomatic posts in Africa, compared to Moscow's twenty-six. However, Chinese-supported subversive activities in Malawi, Zambia, Congo (Leopoldville), and other new states in 1964 aroused the hostility of numerous African leaders. It is therefore too early to assess Peking's prospects for the future. Having burned their fingers, the Chinese, like the Russians and Americans, may move more warily in the future.

NATO has always been under fire in Africa. That is so only partly because Communist and Communist-front organizations make NATO a major target for anti-imperialist resolutions. More important is the animosity aroused in Africa by the use of NATO weapons against Africans, formerly by France in North Africa, and later by Portugal in Angola, Mozambique, and Portuguese Guinea. At the Addis Ababa Summit Conference in May, 1963, Africa's leaders issued a resolution warning "the allies of colonial powers that they must choose between their friendship for the African peoples and their support of powers that oppress African peoples." As long as Portugal retains its African territories, NATO will suffer from the stigma of being a "weapon of Western imperialism." That could become even more true, now that the OAU's Liberation Committee has made Portuguese Africa the first target in its campaign against foreign rule and white supremacy in southern Africa. Conversely, when the Portuguese territories do become independent states, NATO might be viewed less negatively by Africans, some of whom might become more sympathetic to the case for NATO as a mechanism for maintaining international stability. Independence for Portuguese Africa would also take away from the Chinese and Russians a major issue for exploitation in the Cold War.

In any event, African issues will continue to cause friction between Portugal and other NATO powers. The attitude of President de Gaulle within NATO and toward the U.N., as well as his policy of supplying arms to whites in southern Africa, is another source of friction among NATO powers; it could also undermine France's good relations with the leaders of its former African territories.

CONFLICTS BETWEEN AFRICAN STATES AND THE GREAT POWERS

Finally, despite the speed of decolonization, there are numerous disputes between the new African states and the great powers. These controversies revolve around three main issues: nonalignment, neocolonialism, and white supremacy in Southern Africa.

Friction over Africa's insistence on nonalignment with either bloc in the Cold War has been an irritant ever since John Foster Dulles termed neutralism immoral. The Dulles concept was soon abandoned, and official statements now proclaim American respect for nonalignment. But U.S. Government officials still take offense when militant leaders, notably Nasser and Nkrumah, assume positions that coincide with Soviet efforts to reduce Western influence in Africa.

The role of nonalignment in Africa therefore merits a brief reassessment. In such an analysis, it is important to strike a proper balance between the bias of the Cold War specialist and that of the specialist on Africa regarding the nature of the ideological struggle. To many Sino-Sovietologists, the ideological struggle is the struggle between Communism and democracy. The Africanist does not deny the importance of the Cold War, but he is more impressed by the fact that, in the minds of Africans, the Cold War is not at all the key issue. In their quest for a unique ideology, Africans strive to establish their own balance between new and old forms of society, of culture, of religion, and of development. The Africanist is acutely aware of this African ideological struggle and it conditions his attitude toward nonalignment. While the Cold

War specialist tends to call nonalignment "a function of bipolarity," the Africanist regards it as a manifestation of Africanism.

All African states, with the exception of the Republic of South Africa are, by their own definition, nonaligned in the Cold War. When they approved the Charter of the Organization of African Unity, they agreed in Article III, Section 7 to "a policy of nonalignment with regard to all blocs." Despite their declarations of nonalignment, however, African states actually do participate in three broad types of alliances and alignments. The first of these are their own regional and intra-African groupings which are outside the two major power groups. The second type are bilateral and multilateral military arrangements between African states and external powers. These include defense agreements, military base agreements, and military assistance programs. Thirteen African states have defense accords with non-African powers: eleven of the former French territories with France, Liberia with the United States, and Libya with the United Kingdom. These same states and a few others also have military base agreements with France, Britain, and the United States. In the area of military assistance, certain states have preferred to have only one or two principle sources of military aid and training, while others have chosen to diversify their aid sources in order to emphasize their nonalignment.

A third type of African alignment with political significance involves nonmilitary ties with external powers. Most important among them are the many economic and technical ties between the fledgling states and their former metropoles. More ideological in character are the links between African and Asian states through the series of Bandung and Belgrade conferences of Afro-Asian governments, as well as the nongovernmental Afro-Asian Peoples Solidarity Organization.

As a manifestation of Africanism, nonalignment is closely related to African nationalism and Pan-Africanism, and to the fear of neocolonialism and Balkanization. However, the spectrum of nonalignment covers a wide range of attitudes toward the Cold War, and positions shift from time to time for tactical reasons, based on either domestic or external considerations. Despite their close ties with France, however, the leaders of the former French territories find it politically important to say that their policy is not to take sides in the Cold War, but to attempt to "reconcile the sides." As President Senghor of Senegal expressed it on March 18, 1963, even before the Summit Conference in Addis Ababa, "In the area of foreign policy, we define ourselves by nonalignment."

It is true that President Habib Bourguiba of Tunisia, in a notable speech in July, 1958, used the word "pro-Western" to describe his foreign policy. But at the Belgrade Conference of Nonaligned Countries in September, 1961, he declared that "nonalignment has been a fundamental element of our policy for many years." Egypt's President Nasser puts it more colorfully: "I will not become the stooge or satellite or pawn or hireling of anybody." President Julius Nyerere gives us a subtle insight when he declares that Tanzania is unwilling to have "a friendly country choosing enemies for us." Sylvanus Olympio, the late President of Togo who was one of Africa's ablest leaders, illuminated still another aspect of nonalignment when he said, "We have so much to ask for and so little to bargain with." And President Nkrumah refused to associate Ghana with the Common Market of the European Economic Community partly because, he said, such association would have jeopardized Ghana's nonalignment.

None of these declarations, however, clarifies the complex attitudes that underlie nonalignment, so let us probe a little deeper into their causes. These attitudes were sharply expressed in an interesting confrontation between Africans and Sino-Sovietologists and other Cold War specialists at an international conference on "The Nonaligned Afro-Asian Countries in a Divided World" held in Athens, in September, 1962.

When the Sino-Sovietologists warned them of the threat of Soviet imperialism, the African participants were unimpressed. They emphasized that the danger they know comes from their own personal experience with the colonialism of the past and the neo-colonialism of the present. In fact, they contended, Westerners had better stop exaggerating the Soviet threat to Africa. A Nigerian member of the staff of the University of Ibadan declared that he and many others no longer listen to any foreign broadcasts except those of the BBC, because they are sick of the Cold War propaganda of both the Voice of America and Radio Moscow. A

Ugandan faculty member at the University College of East Africa warned that the Soviet Union is asking the right questions about Africa. The West, he said, instead of saying that Western colonialism has its good aspects and that Soviet colonialism is bad, should start trying to answer the questions the Russians are asking. *Anyone* who interests himself in *our* problems, he added, is our friend. He reminded the group that Britain allied itself with the Soviet Union to fight a common problem in World War II, and affirmed that Africans would likewise be willing to work with the Russians until Africans are free in Rhodesia, the Portuguese colonies, and South Africa. Westerners are too impatient, he said. If the Soviet Union ever really threatens Africa's hard-won independence, Africa will turn to the West quickly enough.

A distinguished Nigerian lawyer, who was more conservative, answered in still another way. It is true, he said, that we do not know the Russians, but we do know the West, and our long life under foreign rule unfortunately taught us to believe that we cannot trust the West. *Our distrust of our former rulers is the basic cause of our nonalignment.* If we commit ourselves, he concluded, it will be to ideas—meaning the ideas of human freedom and dignity—not to the *West*. And a Ghanaian professor attacked the Marxist theory of historical materialism as imperialist because "it sees in Europe the key to African history. It does not see Africa as Africans see it."

The African participants were more pragmatic than moralistic in arguing the case for nonalignment. They based the case for nonalignment squarely on the doctrine of national interest. A professor from Sierra Leone who teaches at the University of Nigeria at Nsukka compared the nationalist views of the founding fathers of the United States with those of African leaders today, showing how both wanted (1) no entangling alliances, (2) fewer trade restrictions, (3) rapid economic development and industrialization, (4) the full and free exercise of the right of sovereignty, (5) the withdrawal of foreign governments from their continent, and (6) a hemispheric association of states.

Cold War specialists sometimes argue that the basic cause of nonalignment lies in its potentialities for "blackmailing" both the Western and Soviet powers for economic aid (although these powers never think of themselves as guilty of "bribery" when they try to buy friends with aid). It is true that Africans are quite pragmatic in stating that they want aid from both sides in order to achieve their major objective of rapid economic development. However, this is obviously not the original cause of nonalignment. When Nehru set the tone of nonalignment back in 1947, the Cold War competition to aid Asia and Africa had not yet begun. It was not until 1953 that the Soviet Union began to give assistance to Asia, and not until 1958 that it began to aid Africa (aside from military help to Egypt in 1955).

"Neocolonialism" is a second source of friction between African states and great powers. An understanding of the fear of neocolonialism also helps to explain the desire for nonalignment. As defined by its foremost critic, Kwame Nkrumah, neocolonialism is "political independence minus economic independence." Nkrumah pinpointed its relationship to nonalignment when he attacked the European Common Market as a neocolonialist form of "collective colonialism" in a speech on June 4, 1962, to a group of freedom fighters being trained in Ghana. Above all, he said, African states entering the Common Market "will lose their option of nonalignment and find themselves dragged into the diplomacy of imperialist cold war politics. . . ."

The close economic, technical, educational, and cultural links between African states and their former metropoles are actually not at all difficult to reconcile with the political posture of nonalignment. It is a matter of psychology. Perhaps because of these continuing ties with the West, Africans feel all the more need to demonstrate their political independence by emphasizing their nonalignment. That is also why they brand many of these relationships as neocolonialism. It is a kind of psychological compensation for their inability to get rid of all the *old world* of colonial relationships in their *new world* of freedom.

One must acknowledge, however, that it is more than just a psychological matter. The economic reality of Africa's continuing dependence on the West cannot be denied. In his book *The African Nations and World Solidarity*, the former Senegalese Prime Minister Mamadou Dia cites examples in Eastern Europe, as well as in the Middle East and North Africa, to support his contention that "economic neocolonialism" is "the successor of classical imperialism." In his view, the only way to escape Balkanization and neocolonialism is "a true interregionalization of economies" and the ending of "the hegemony of guiding nations." In such a blend of economics and psychology, Pan-African movements appear as escape routes from neocolonialism.

The third and by far the most dangerous of the changing conflict patterns between African states and the great powers is the rising African bitterness against whites in Rhodesia, Angola, Mozambique, and above all, South Africa. Although basically a conflict between South Africa and the rest of Africa, what to do about South Africa is becoming a conflict with mounting racial overtones between African states and the great powers. Lord Caradon, the leader of the British Labour Government's delegation to the United Nations is an eloquent exponent of the thesis that mankind's greatest danger is the threat of a world-wide racial war between white and nonwhite peoples. In Lord Caradon's view, South Africa is the fuse that could set off the explosion.

The determination of African leaders to rid the continent of Portuguese rule, and to overthrow the white supremacy governments in Rhodesia and South Africa, is the most obvious, consistent, and all-embracing common denominator of African foreign policies. Since the OAU's Liberation Committee is subsidizing and otherwise aiding revolutionaries in Portuguese territories, Rhodesia, and South Africa, some observers ask whether the OAU is not an alliance for aggression rather than defense. Africans respond that the original seizures of African territories by invaders from Europe were and remain illegal acts of aggression and that the OAU's Liberation Committee is only continuing the defense of Africa against the aggressors. In a Tanzanian view,

> During the last war America supported resistance movements in occupied territories. Our position is not different just because the occupation took place many years ago. In the same way that freed countries immediately became part of the general war effort for the freedom of Europe, so we in Tanganyika . . . Uganda, Congo, Ghana and so on must carry the fight forward until the whole of Africa is free.[3]

[3] *Revolution,* Dar es Salaam, I, Nos. 4–5 (August–September, 1963), 113–14.

In any event, whether the OAU is an offensive or defensive alliance, the most powerful psychological force holding it together is the absolute unity of the member states against foreign rule and white supremacy anywhere in Africa. South Africa's policy of apartheid is therefore doomed to remain "a cancer gnawing at world peace and tranquility," to use a phrase once applied to the U.N. by South African Prime Minister D. F. Malan. In the words of Louis Rakotomalala, a U.N. spokesman of the conservative Malagasy Government:

> To the Government of South Africa . . . we very frankly say: "This Liberation will be carried out—with you, against you, or without you. . . . Let not this appeal fall on deaf ears, because it is no longer 12 million coloured men, unarmed and defenseless, that stand before you: It is 200 million Africans . . . determined to free their brethren."[4]

In their U.N. battles against apartheid, Africans and Asians thus place a higher priority on the human rights provision of the Charter than they do on the preservation of peace. In Africa, the longer the struggle lasts, the more bitter and bloody and openly racist it will become. And the longer South Africa's major trading partners embitter Africans by refusing to intervene on the side of the new states, the more vulnerable the Western position in Africa will become. By 1963, Portugal had 40,000 to 50,000 white troops in Angola, 20,000 in Mozambique, and 6,000 in Portuguese Guinea. In South Africa, a great build-up of arms and armies in recent years now enables the government to put perhaps 250,000 white troops and citizen-force trainees into the field. In such circumstances, it becomes less and less likely that the new states of middle Africa will find it practicable to limit their own armaments. On the contrary, they will be under pressure not only to increase their armaments, but to ensure their supply lines by diversifying the sources from which they obtain arms.

However, the extent to which the OAU states can sustain a long effort against the white redoubt in Southern Africa is problematical. How far will each state go in its fight against apartheid? Will it jeopardize its development plans by actually carrying out the

---

[4] Cited in *United Nations Review*, August–September, 1963, p. 21.

OAU's projected secondary boycotts against the ships and planes of third countries doing business with South Africa? Will Africans go further than this and discriminate against international firms in tropical Africa, if those firms do business in South Africa? Presumably, Africans are not yet sure of the answers to all these questions. While it may be true that many African leaders are not as passionate as their words suggest, the constant repetition of the slogan that "None of us is free until all are free" is nonetheless building up a social myth that could prove stronger than reality. In the imagery of President Sékou Touré of Guinea, Africa is like a human body—if one finger is cut, the whole body feels the pain.

The Underlying Inclination Toward Radicalism

Among numerous attempts to classify African states in recent years, the most common system divides them into radical, moderate, and conservative camps. These categories are useful to policymakers in Washington who concentrate primarily on Cold War problems. But, for at least two reasons, they can become a trap for loose thinking. In the first place, African states shift their positions on this radical-to-conservative spectrum so often that at best, its validity is poor. In fact, when Westerners stereotype an African state as "moderate," "good," "friendly," or "pro-Western," they tend to force its leaders to shift their positions in order to escape this Western accolade.

More important, however, is the underlying fact that all African states are revisionist "by necessity, not by ideology," as one of Tunisia's leaders remarked to me in February, 1965. Since the United States is rich, he said, it must naturally be a *status quo* power in order to preserve its riches; conversely, since Tunisia is poor it must be a *revisionist* power in order to improve the life of its people. The style of Ghana's leaders is at present more militant than that of Tunisia's, he added, but this does not mean that Ghana is more revisionist than Tunisia. For the problems and aspirations of the two countries are identical.

It is no doubt true that Africa has far more conservatives than radicals, mainly the rural people who cling to the old ways. In fact, from the point of view of the historian, every revolution leaves more of the old ways and beliefs intact than it changes. But Africa's radicals are concentrated in the leadership elite, the "new men" of rising expectations who are trying to remake Africa. In one sense, it might be argued that the basic conflict pattern is one of neither necessity nor ideology but simply the struggle of the new men to induce their countrymen to change their ways.

In international relations, however, the outside world has to deal with the new leaders. Although the short-term tactics of some African leaders are less militant than the methods of others, the internal dynamics of the countries will impel them sooner or later toward radical methods of tackling the basic political, economic, social, and educational problems that have continued to plague them after independence. An observer who grasps this fact will not be surprised when allegedly moderate states suddenly behave like radicals.

In the climate of opinion in the West, the key words are moderation, stability, and orderly progress. Most Westerners are therefore out of tune with the radical spirit of Africa's leaders and are unable to view it with the necessary understanding. This is the greatest of all our problems in learning to deal with the new states of Africa.

II

National Interest and Ideology

I. WILLIAM ZARTMAN

Motivational studies are quagmires of uncertainty. The ground between the announced reasons and the "real" reasons for action is marshy, and, while the public reasons may be manifestly political or justificative in nature, an attempt to find the hidden, private, or even subconscious motives can lead the student into the role of psychoanalyst, father confessor, divine, or simply frustrated hairsplitter. He is obliged to judge the choice of criteria on the basis of indirect evidence: justifications given, policies adopted, decision-making processes involved, all joined together with insight and "right reason." The greatest problem for the analyst lies in the need to keep an academic neutrality toward value systems and criteria used by the subjects of his study.

The reader's greatest problem will be to remember continually that this is a motivational study. A treatment of ideology and interest, in fact a treatment of any determinants of foreign policy, is not a study of acts but of reasons for acting, not a study of policy but of decision-making.[1] A state acting for ideological rea-

[1] A question asked during the conference discussion illustrates the difference. Someone asked whether Freetown's decision to recognize Peking was based on national interest or on ideology. The policy itself does not take us very far toward an answer to the question; what must be known above all are the criteria, motives, and thoughts of the decision-makers that went into making the decision.

sons may make the same decision as a state acting for reasons of interest, or the same act may be decided for mixed reasons. A state acting for reasons of national interest may not necessarily act "in the national interest," depending on who is evaluating that interest and on how successfully the policy has been conceived and carried out.

There are other difficulties in such a study. One is the problem of overlapping categories. National interest involves considerations of ideology, but ideology may be a way of perceiving the national interest. Yet the two are not the same. The problem here will be to make the difference clear while accounting for the overlap. There is the opposite danger of unreal extremes. No state operates entirely on the basis of ideology; such a policy would be one of self-abnegation and would run the risk of suicide. But neither do states act only on the basis of national interest; even if they do not have an ideology, they are unlikely to avoid the influence of domestic politics, culture, external or other pressures. Since most states act for a confusion of reasons, an attempt to strain the mud out of the waters does not necessarily help an analysis of the currents.

I

The old order has changed. During the last three-quarters of a century, Africa has been part of the Europe-centered world system of international relations. African territories were not members in their own right, but only as colonial appendages to European states. The colonial system of international relations played two important roles in African relations. Besides introducing modernization to Africa, European states served as Africa's policemen, keeping order within vast expanses of colonial territories. They also governed Africa in their own interests; when their order-keeping functions broke down, the wars that they sponsored were extensions of European power conflicts, of little interest to Africans.

Now the colonial system is gone, and with it the security and interest roles that the European states played. Africa is responsible for its own order and security; its states can consider their own interests as a guide to their policies; they also have a role to play in determining the new system of international relations. In regard to the latter role, a number of possibilities are open. African states can seek full membership in the old, but expanded, multi-state system. They can participate in a world-wide bipolar bloc system structured on competing foreign ideologies. They can aspire to a new universal system of world government, based either on a new concept of equality of members or on the old rules governing competition between powers. Or they can seek to create a new system that will assure the values of dignity, justice, and well-being of all members.

Yet Africa is in a poor position to play any of those roles. In the new states, formal independence has been achieved, the legal myths of sovereignty have been donned, and national elites are now in the position of making their own decisions for their own reasons. But there is no structure behind the legal façade. The nation is inchoate, the territorial extent of government control is indefinite, political skills are rare, and elites are small. The population has been led to expect the good things of modern life (including security, well-being, and national identity), but the absolute number of people in the state, the relative proportion of the people that have raised their expectations, and the expectations themselves are all growing faster than the means—public or private—of satisfaction. The governmental elites are under pressure to fill in the structure behind the façade of sovereignty, lest the façade come tumbling down and their heads with it.

Unfortunately, the inadequacy is compounded by the fact that underdevelopment includes not only material insufficiency and dissatisfaction but also the means of overcoming them. The absence of effective authority is a major characteristic of underdevelopment. States lack not only the elements of national power but also the capacity to build up these elements, at least in the short run. Without authority and control, development cannot be accomplished; without development, the basis of power is largely absent. The absence of effective authority is felt at every turn. It is hard to perceive and plan opportunities for development; where such opportunities are visible, the means of exploiting them are scarce. It is hard to make decisions under conflicting pressures and harder to execute and enforce decisions when made; the writ of the government often shades into ineffectiveness outside the capital and sometimes even outside the presidential palace. It is hard to defend the external interests and security of the state when one's voice is small and when one is listened to only for the sake of politeness or sentiment, in a world arena where, ultimately, the clangor of powerful sabers makes small voices hard to hear. In sum, in their moment of greatest need and opportunity, as the old order shows signs of crumbling, African states have little control over their own security and environment.

With few exceptions, the new states of Africa have been in no danger of attack. Yet, in a general sense, their very existence and stability are far more tenuous than the small number of incidents and symptoms of their early life would indicate. Insecurity is endemic, if not always specific. The threats are not external as much as internal. Yet the threats—whether they be political, economic, or social—are troublesome for governments to admit publicly, difficult to combat effectively or to identify precisely. Although some leaders may face up to the internal problems realistically, the magnitude of the problems and the elusiveness of their sources constitute a temptation to view the insecurity in external terms. The temptation and the confusion are compounded in Africa by another characteristic of the insecurity: It refers to the political more than to the territorial aspect of the state. The country is not in danger of attack or conquest as much as the government is in danger of overthrow or collapse.

In such a situation, the African states are primarily preoccupied with development and nation-building. If the nation itself can be defined as "a group of people who feel themselves to be a nation," nationalism can be characterized as the efforts of men striving to build a nation. Although the task is unending, a beginning must be made. On the one hand, there is a pressing need to solve problems, essentially technical in nature, that deprive the state of its power to act independently. The state seeks to protect, augment, and diversify its internal economy and its foreign trade, protect its frontiers, educate and employ its people, and conduct the many other activities that allow it a freedom of choice and a variety of means to carry out its policies. It must satisfy its growing population's rising expectations, lest that revolution turn instead into a revolution of failing satisfactions. In brief, it must turn to the task of constructing a state, with a possibility of choosing among alternative actions that makes independence a reality. On the other hand, there is an equally pressing need to create solidarity, in order to keep the state going while the problems await solution. State leadership must justify its claim to authority by legitimizing its own position. It must unite its people in a feeling of nationhood, create a spirit of dignity and a mental emancipation to replace the colonial past, and nurture the enthusiasm that will make the efforts and sacrifices of development bearable. In sum, it must turn to the task of building a nation, with the feelings of identity that also make independence a reality.

Optimally, the two tasks go hand in hand. But because of the pressures of the moment and the limited attention and resources available, priorities must be established. Criteria for the problem-solvers and the solidarity-makers differ, and even conflict in some cases.[2] The problem-solvers seek to overcome directly the problems of underdevelopment, which they see as the main cause of their country's weakness, instability, and disorganization; their view has been patterned after modern governmental ideas, in which the state is a problem-solving mechanism, rather than after the traditional view of government employment as something merely to be enjoyed. The solidarity-makers seek to consolidate their position and unite their nation, for they regard disunity and disorganization as the biggest barriers to development and complete independence; they feel their view was vindicated by their experiences in achieving formal independence, when they organized their people to political action—the only means of power available against the colonial rulers—and conquered a state. Both problem-solvers and solidarity-makers, then, are reacting to the needs and pressures of their situation, as they see it.

[2] The two categories come from Herbert Feith, *The Decline of Constitutional Democracy in Indonesia* (Ithaca, N.Y.: Cornell University Press, 1962), and are extended by Donald E. Weatherbee, "Indonesia's Revolutionary Ideology" (Columbia, S.C.: Institute of International Studies, 1965; mimeographed Colloquium on Political Strategy paper). Lawrence Radway's "goal-achievement" and "system-maintenance" are less clear; see K. H. Silvert (ed.), *Discussion at Bellagio* (New York: American Universities Field Staff, 1964), p. 86.

Such reactions to insecurity can be analyzed as being adaptive or maladaptive; that is, the state can accept the general environment and attempt to find its place within it, or it can reject the environment and try to change it. One response seeks security within the present state system by overcoming internal weaknesses and increasing state power; the other sees only insecurity as long as the present order continues. (Note that "adaptive" and "maladaptive" as used here are not synonyms of "good" and "bad," but merely indicate an attitude toward the environment within which the state finds itself.) The first attitude uses national interest as its criterion for action, the second is ideological.[3] Both seek an answer to the insecurity of the state.

II

The extreme case of national-interest foreign policy is Realpolitik, by which foreign relations are carried out among states seeking to maximize their security, regardless of ideological considerations. In this case, the state uses its policy to secure values or objects that form the basic components of its definition of itself. While in past eras and other areas, this "self" may have been conceived simply in terms of the physical integrity and territorial independence of land and people, in the twentieth-century Cold War world, other values have been added. In a schematic sense, the image of the self includes three elements: the physical state (territory and people), its way of life, and its standard of living (welfare). These elements make up the national interest. The concept of national interest, however, has never been susceptible of a definition so precise that it tells the state exactly where its security lies, how its component elements should be defined or determined, or what particular policies to adopt. It does not provide a complete description of the process of policy-making and execution; it cannot, therefore, tell anything about the success of a policy, and, conversely, the outcome of the policy does not determine the reasons for its choice. The concept can only provide a general criterion for action.

[3] Many examples in the following discussion draw on events in North and West Africa. An excellent case study that applies similar concepts to another part of the continent is Joseph S. Nye, Jr., *Pan-Africanism and East African Federation* (Cambridge, Mass.: Harvard University Press, 1965).

Nevertheless, with the use of the national-interest criterion, there is an attempt to account for the economic and physical needs of the society. It is the response to reality of the nationalist who above all seeks to solve the material problems of his state.

National-interest policy is geared to the perceived good of the *state;* it does not seek to transfer allegiance and justification to a larger unit, such as region, race, creed, or continent. "A nationalist is one who gives the Nation first place in the hierarchy of political values and who, in doing this, evaluates political events as a function of the national interest"—the definition of a 1962 Ivory Coast study group. To some extent, the national-interest approach is a product of the situation in which African leaders find themselves. No matter how narrow its real base, African national leadership is under pressure to justify its actions in terms of national considerations. The necessity is in part self-imposed, since the ruling party lives by the myth that it acts in the name of all the people, that its goals are for the good of all the people, and that its leader incarnates the new nation as the tribal chief incarnated the traditional one. However, at the current stage of development of national-interest ideas, the accent is primarily on the first word of the term. The focus is national, with little conception of the specific interests involved. National interest has mainly a negative implication, i.e., that policies shall no longer be decided on the basis of colonial, metropolitan, regional, tribal, or class interests. Thus, the very use of the phrase and its implied meaning push the concept onto a high level of generalization, away from having any specific content or useful value as a guide for action.

Appreciation of the national interest depends on both awareness and perception—awareness of the need of policy to consider the well-being and security of the state and to find opportunities to do so, and perception or interpretation of the state's concept of itself and of challenges to it. There is no single "correct" perception of the national interest (although there is a presupposition that state decision-makers have a more valid perception of these components than their critics or their analysts, just as a man knows better than his doctor when he is hungry). Furthermore, it is in the nature of states' interest to clash. The national interest of both Somalia and Ethiopia may or may not cover Ogaden, depending on equally "valid" supporting arguments adduced by either side; Dahomeyans and Mauritanians have consistently followed foreign policies that preserve their "personalities," while their neighbors have sought to assure the same value by offering policies of integration and amalgamation; Félix Houphouet-Boigny and Sékou Touré obviously put welfare on very different levels in their hierarchy of foreign-policy criteria in 1958 and 1959, and Houphouet-Boigny and Kwame Nkrumah have differed widely on the best way to attain development since 1957, when they wagered on which economy would show the greatest growth in the following decade. Policy-makers agree only on the fact that certain components are the minimum values to be secured by foreign policy. They do not agree on the relative position of one value vis-à-vis another—that is, which value shall be sacrificed in a pinch; there is no consensus on how the values are to be interpreted. Finally, they cannot be expected to agree on the nature of the threats to the national interest or, a fortiori, on the means of combating them. The members of the French-allied regional defense councils, the government of the Congo (Leopoldville), and the eighteen associate members of the European Common Market see in ties with European states a means of assuring the territorial, way-of-life, and welfare components of national interest; Ghana, Algeria, and Egypt disagree.

Perception and awareness depend, in turn, on two interrelated elements that may be termed informational input and intake. The information that is brought to the attention of decision-makers and the degree to which it is integrated into the policy-making have much to do with the effectiveness of national-interest criteria. In the Ivory Coast, a 1962 party seminar held a discussion on "A Methodology for Action by Men in Posts of Political Responsibility" and outlined three objectives: "(1) to learn the rational use of materials; (2) to prepare an inventory of political, institutional, economic, and social data; and (3) to define the specifically Ivoirien context, from which it will be possible to establish rational, objective criteria of evaluation and judgment as a valid basis for action." Although African leaders are highly knowledgeable about the politics of their country and its social characteristics, many of them are uninformed about its potential resources, its developmental possibilities, and the ways of meeting its material needs. Frequently, such information does not exist. There is little information and less agreement on methods of agricultural improvement, on designs for transportation systems, on the location of some raw materials, and on possibilities of market development. Yet, both information and agreement are necessary for rational cooperation toward common exploitation of resources and toward effective aid projects, as well as for building up the power base and establishing policy alternatives of states.

Basic political and economic information about foreign-policy operations areas is also lacking. Foreign ministries generally are small, and their desk officers usually depend on a newspaper-clipping file; since the desk officer usually covers a continent and not a country, his territory is as vast as his sources of information are meager. The situation is complicated by the political nature of information in some countries. Many of the better foreign newspapers are regarded with suspicion because of their European origins; often a party line on the interpretation of events prevents information from a large number of varying sources from being fully assimilated. Ghana, with a peculiar relation existing between the press and the government, is a striking example: Newspapers present a narrowly orthodox interpretation of African events; Ghanaian leaders feel that they speak for the "true African" interpretation of policy, and they become prisoners of their own misinformation. Policy papers are little used in West Africa; telephone communication and personal conversations are preferred to written memoranda. It is doubtful, too, if the few studies that do exist are always carefully read by those who need to act on them.

Moreover, technical intelligence that is available is put in a bad operating environment by the penchant of African heads of state for handling foreign policy personally, inviting all the dangers of misinformation on details that are inherent in summitry. Intra-African relations tend to be personal relations among heads of state, where personal reactions prevail. Any observer will perceive facts in the light of his own experience, but the great diversity in Africa—and, indeed, in the world—makes this frame of reference inadequate for an understanding of foreign-policy problems even within Africa, the myth of African cultural unity notwithstanding.

Another reason for (and result of) the absence of national-interest criteria is that policies often are adopted on an *ad hoc* basis, with decisions made only as problems are posed and with little consideration given to future consequences or to the implementation of details. The many important suggestions for policy made in conferences and communiqués—African common market, African assembly, common Saharan or riverine exploitation, common diplomatic representation, coordination of legislation and services, to name a few—have for the most part remained not only unrealized but unstudied. Several of the African alliances and groups themselves have appeared and disappeared without any real attempt to set up institutions, make them work, and attack common problems.

All these weaknesses have hampered awareness and perception of the importance of national interest. Even if input sources and intake channels are open, however, there are other barriers to action in national-interest terms. It is difficult to attain an end if the means are absent. In Africa, the classical elements of state power are noticeably weak. Area is especially illusory, since the largest states are largely desert or rain forest and the land is generally poor. Population figures must be tempered by considerations of illiteracy, heterogeneity, underemployment, ruralism, and apathy; the 55 million people of Africa's most populous state, Nigeria, both cause problems and represent potential but do not yet give power. Military strength is low in both absolute and relative terms, and is further depleted by domestic preoccupations, inefficiency, and terrain. Economic development is the goal, not the reality, of African politics; the fact that several states have per capita incomes between $150 and $225, while the incomes of most of the rest are between $40 and $85, does not give the richer states enough of an edge to provide durable power.

Of all the classical elements on which state power is based, only access to means of communication plays some importance. Coastal states that control inland countries' outlets to the sea and states that lie astride rivers or rail lines enjoy a certain position of influence. However, power and susceptibility to pressure are two sides of the same coin in this case; inland states or states with eccentric regions—Tindouf in Algeria, Nzérékoré in Guinea, Katanga in the

Congo—need good relations with a maritime neighbor, but port states need good relations with a hinterland area.

In addition to the elements of state power, the channels for exercising power are only rudimentary. Power can be exercised in many ways: directly between individuals, on the basis of personality or pleas; indirectly between individuals, through threats, slogans, purchase, or reason; indirectly between decision-making elites, through public opinion or pressure groups; or directly between states, through use of sanctions and force. All but the first category involve the use of real or implied gratifications or deprivations. In Africa, the instruments of power and policy by which gratifications and deprivations can be exercised are slim indeed. Approbation can be extended or withheld (justifying slogans can be used to condemn or to condone); trade routes can be cut and products can be withheld; military threats can be made, with varying degrees of credibility. But the list stops there. Sanctions and force are either disallowed or impractical; public opinion and pressure groups have little weight in the decision-making process and foreign leaders frequently have little access to them; purchase and reason, in a bargaining process, are rarely used, in the absence of national-interest criteria to which they can be applied, making compromise a rarity. Decision-making tends to be an uncomplex, personal process, and channels of communication between decision-making elites are not rich in diversification. Even if the national interest is perceived, it is pursued only with difficulty.

III

Ideology is also a response to reality. In the new African states, the lack of consensus, legitimacy, authority, and unity is often the most pressing problem, and the one that the problem-solvers cannot handle. The old order—tribal and colonial—and the old myths have been destroyed or have proved inadequate to handle or explain the new situation. Specifically, the nation in search of its identity, the people in search of material satisfactions, and the state in search of its security, all want to know why power to achieve their goals is lacking, how the necessary means can be attained, and what will be the shape of the future order that they can expect. Ideology attempts to answer these questions when old explanations have failed. This characterization brings out three important aspects of the phenomenon.

First, it suggests that ideology is a situational phenomenon, associated with societal change. Ideologies do not create revolutions; if a new ideology appeared upon a scene where stability and harmony existed within the society and polity, where no drastic changes threatened the established order, and where existing myths were adequate to support that order, it would be a seed on stony ground. Instead, ideologies appear when the breakdown of a society and its myths has already begun. It is the intellectuals' response to the situation, designed to help further the breakdown and guide society into a new order. During the revolution, the ideology is under pressure to remain pure. It is the ideal that is to guide the change, and as such it dares not compromise with the reality it seeks to alter until it has accomplished its purpose. Since, at this stage, it is prescriptive, ideology is anti-reality, and is under continual internal pressure, imposed by its own nature, to remain so.

As time passes, the situation changes. The revolution is over, either won or worn-out, and a new order has been imposed. If the upheaval has resulted in an order that differs from the one prescribed by the ideology, and a new equilibrium has been created by forces that are stronger than the ideology, the prescriptive ideals remain under pressure to retain their purity, but they become voices in the wilderness, unable to find support. If, on the other hand, the ideology has so influenced the current of events that it becomes the dominant myth of the new order, it loses much of its purity and its anti-reality nature. It becomes a conservative influence instead of a force for change. In such a situation, however, reality usually approximates the ideal; and the ideal shapes itself to fit the new reality. A compromise is achieved. The ideology "accepts" the reality, cutting corners that its proponents deem minor, correcting errors where its advocates see the inadequacy of their former descriptions. Now, the ideology is under pressure to compromise if it is to achieve the position of an official myth. (Rarely, in fact, will all the goals prescribed by the former ideal be achieved by the new order.) Conversely, it is under less pressure to retain its militancy and its insistence on orthodoxy, since a new stability has been found and opposing forces have been defeated or have met in truce. Purism tends to be dropped. Descriptively, ideology now deals with a situational reality that it approves and supports, and must change its revolutionary-idealist nature if it is to continue to receive credence and acceptance in the new situation. The second implication of ideology's character, then, is that eventually it must grapple with reality and that it generally gives way in the encounter.

The third point concerns ideology's role as an explanation. Ideology both prescribes and describes, as seen, its twin functions intertwined to provide satisfying answers to the political and psychological needs of the society. It answers those needs in three ways: it consolidates, it identifies, and it assures. In consolidating, it fills the needs of the solidarity-makers, who are looking for a way to legitimize their authority and unite their nation. The ideology provides something in which to believe, a plausible explanation of events as old myths are destroyed. The element of faith is important: The pressure of the revolutionary situation does not allow time for experiments and demonstrations, but rather obliges the ideology to explain by logic and symbols; on this basis it must be believed. To the propagators, it gives authority, for they have the correct interpretation of events; their power is legitimized by their ability to explain. To the true believer, it gives a sense of unity and solidarity, as it creates a community of faith. Once this solidarity is posited, it becomes a value to defend, thus legitimizing not only authority but also its ultimate attribute—the use of force—to assure adherence to the ideology. (More frequently, however, ideology is an alternative to coercion, since compliance is achieved by indoctrination and solidarity, instead of by compulsion and obedience.) Furthermore, if ideology provides the correct interpretation of events, it also justifies the formulation of policy based on its tenets and creates ties of solidarity and means of communication outside the state with other communities of believers, in power or out of power. Since the ideology legitimizes but also transcends the state, it becomes the value to be defended in foreign policy, as indeed in domestic politics.

In identifying, the ideology reinforces its consolidating function. Analyses of the new nations have often been based on the preoccupying search for identity. In the absence of other senses of belonging—particularly the sense of nationhood, which is longer in developing—ideological solidarity provides an answer to this search. Furthermore, ideology expresses the resentments and rejections of its adherents—its correctness in isolating these feelings and its plausibility in explaining their cause and remedy enhancing its claim to being the true faith. The identity function of ideology tells not only who I am but also who are, and who are not, my brothers. Internally, it permits the identification of the enemies of society—a prelude to their destruction. Externally, it distinguishes friend from foe with the neatness of a password. It tells who can be trusted, since it examines their objective situation as well as their subjective reactions. This aspect of identity in turn is vital to the solidarity function and to the whole strength of the ideology. As long as enemies exist, solidarity is necessary; as long as the enemy is common, solidarity is possible. As long as a plausible source of evil can be identified, the ideology retains its claim to correctness and the solidarity-makers their claim to authority. Finally, the identification function justifies policy. The existentialist exhortation to define oneself through action expresses the pressure on the ideologues to take the initiative, promote the faith, test the enemy, help the brothers, and generally carry out a policy of activism and leadership in domestic and foreign affairs.

In assuring, ideology maintains solidarity and identity and promotes its own durability. Ideology not only rationalizes, explaining the reasons for the present situation; it also points the way to the future goal. In a time of uncertainty and upheaval, ideology serves both as a lifebuoy of stability in a maelstrom of change and as a chart that promises safe arrival at the desired goal. It can sanction the rejection of present reality because it assures the way to an acceptable new order, and it can do both because it has identified the wave of the future: It can say things will get worse before they get better because it "knows" they will get better. Assurance of victory justifies both sacrifices and failures. Ideology fills the psychological needs of its adherents by making the present time of crisis livable. "As for us, we stay calm, decided, firmly attached to principles," said Mohammed Yazid in 1959, during the dark days of the Algerian war. "Do you know why? Because we are tomorrow!" As long as the assurance remains credible, the ideologues can impose discipline and even force, demand compliance and even enthusiasm, and create morality. More important, they can justify their own failures and make them bearable, for failure is not the fault of the ideologue, riding the wave of the future; it is the doing of the enemy, who is still powerful enough to divide, delay, and deflect, although of course not destroy, the inevitability. Even an unbroken stream of failures need not be fatal to ideological assurance, at least over the short run; it can convince the believers of the need for greater effort and push them to fanaticism. A few successes, not even at home but among other communities of believers, can increase longevity tremendously.

A value of examining ideology's explanatory role through these three functions is that certain aspects of ideology which have hitherto been viewed through the analyst's own value pattern as aberrations can now be seen as natural and even necessary parts of the phenomenon. An understanding of the consolidation function can avoid the interpretation of ideology as merely a cover for a power struggle among men or among states. Ideology is believed, before it is used. There is simply no evidence that any African leaders are such skillful actors or total liars that they cynically use their ideologies without believing in them;[4] were they to attempt to do so, they would soon find themselves prisoners of their tactics, forced to follow or to break ideological ranks. Of course, disclaiming the interest theory of ideology, according to which beliefs are only a "mask and a weapon" in the struggle for power, does not imply that ideology is the sole motivation. Such single-mindedness is rare, even among believers. Personal interest can well be a motivating factor, frequently disguised with care under ideological slogans. Problems of analysis in such cases are admittedly difficult, particularly since the solidarity-maker may—indeed must—sincerely feel that the fate of the ideology, on which the fate of the society

[4] An exception appears to be Hassan II, who once told U.S. representatives that the American Government would do best to find the most radical leaders in Africa and back them; the superficially and temporarily radical turn of Moroccan foreign policy between 1960 and 1962 reflected this thinking.

depends, hangs on his own success. An even more perplexing ethical dilemma is posed when the leader is required to make an anti-ideological decision in order to save his own power, which he (let us say, sincerely) believes necessary for the ultimate preservation of the ideology and the society. Such dilemmas are characteristic of any ethical system. Painful as they may be to the subject, they are useful to the analyst in showing that both ideological and personal considerations can come into play in a decision.

An understanding of the identification function of ideology can avoid belittling the need for enemies as a mere search for scapegoats. Certainly the enemy has a scapegoat role, but he is not a haphazard object of irrelevant blame; he is crucial to the ideology. The scapegoat is the external source of frustration on which the whole theory is built. He has a satanic role: The single cause of evil, he adopts many forms but has one substance. His nature, correctly identified, prescribes the proper counter-tactics. If he is an encircling capitalist, the response must be to pierce his lines and divide his forces. If he is a dividing, conquering colonialist, the response is to unite, to remove his armies, to control his merchants. From the outside, the enemy infiltrates his agents and utilizes his unregenerate hangers-on. But they are also easily identified, not just by their anti-ideological attitudes, but because they are the ones who are responsible for the troubles and failures. The enemy is not simply an innocent bystander whose name is sullied by the troubled leader as he tries to get off the hook; rather, the ideologue believes that problems are prima facie evidence of the enemy's presence. Hence Modibo Keita felt that there *had* to be colonialist agents among the rebellious Tuareg in northern Mali, not that the revolt resulted from a clash between partial national consolidation and traditional society. Similarly, Nkrumah felt that Tshombe *had* to be a neocolonialist agent, not a man with a different but legitimately African view of interest and world order. Again, it must be remembered that the ideology and its explanations are believed, and the enemy, more than a mere scapegoat, is central to these myths.

Finally, an understanding of the assurance function elucidates ideology's clash with reality and avoids equating "unscientific" with "bad." Ideologues do confuse ideology with science by con-

fusing systematic with experimental, goals with givens, and promises with premises. Their theories are literally working hypotheses,
which, however, they follow instead of testing. From the point of
view of the scientific method, this is indeed a mistake. But to ideologues, consciously or unconsciously, scientificalness has an instru-
mental value, enabling them to consolidate, identify, and assure a
state that is unstable, insecure, and weak. Such things science never
purported to do, and to condemn ideology as being unscientific in
such a situation is as meaningful as condemning opera or poetry for
its lack of objectivity. The same thing is true of ideology's un-
reality. How could it be otherwise? Ideology is an ideal, a satisfying explanation, a societal myth, an assurance of things to come. It
analyzes reality, not as an end, but as a means to political goals. It
seeks to change reality, by throwing its influence against the course
of events. Crane Brinton has shown that "the normal social roles
of realism and idealism are reversed in the acute phases of a revolution." To say ideology deals with reality means only that it must
come to grips with events if it is to maintain its authority. Ideology does not have to be true; it need only be effective. Lastly, to
say that ideology is extrarealistic does not deny that ideology is
itself a reality, a force among many, a cause of action. So-called
realistic explanations of situations and events which omit ideology
because its basis is extrarealistic are ignoring a real ingredient of
the problem.

Against this attempt to outline the nature of ideology, what is
its role in African foreign policy? There are six distinct functions
with reference to external relations, some of them taken directly
from the previous description and others representing specific
applications. Most important is the general use of ideology to perceive events and explain their meanings. To Algeria, the Cuban
revolution is a revolt against American imperialism,[5] and the Congolese Committee of National Liberation (CLN) is a people's up-

---

[5] A judgment, of course, that contains some truth, as do many myths. It is
interesting to note that the Algerian public literacy campaign instructions
took pains to warn against "a too-hasty analogy between that country
[Cuba] and Algeria," particularly in regard to Cuba's "(even relatively) long-
standing independence . . ." *Dossier d'Information* (mimeographed; Algiers:
Commission nationale d'alphabetisation [n.d.]), "Index des questions," p. 4.
In this document, Cuba was referred to as "*semi*-colonial."

rising against Belgian-American attempts at domination. To Ghana, a critical editorial in a British newspaper is not a discussion of specific events in Accra, to be refuted by reference to facts or even justifications; it is rather a colonialist attempt to discredit the Ghanaian regime and so weaken the forces of unity in Africa, and can be properly answered only by exposing the motives of the newspaper. Sometimes the interpretive role of ideology gets in the way, however, and leaves the viewer more perplexed than enlightened. Guinea could not understand how, as Afro-Asian states and ideological brothers of Guinea, India and China could go to war; since, from Guinea's point of view, the conflict must have arisen from a misunderstanding, the matter could be resolved by a cease-fire, withdrawal to positions, and recognition of a convenient line (which happened to be the Chinese proposal).

More specifically, ideology helps identify friends and enemies as a basis for policy. Members of the Union of African States (UAS) could agree on a list of principles, even if largely unimplemented, because they had regimes based on similar ideologies. The three states of the Maghrib were able to concert their plans and actions only to the extent and at the time (1958) that their ideological orientation included common, predominant values (single nationalist movement, accent on liberation, regional unity); ideological similarities and the basis of cooperation fell apart when internal developments and external circumstances changed and affected the three countries differently. Even among the four states of the Entente, there was an ideological element in the choice of partners, reinforced before the establishment of the alliance by the installation of sympathetic regimes in the Ivory Coast's three allies and afterward by the promulgation of constitutions and legislation reflecting the same points of view. Considerations of principle, rather than considerations of interest, are also invoked in the choice of enemies. In nearly every case of bad relations, ideological reasons are cited, although they may or may not be decisive. After their first meeting, in 1957, when Nkrumah and Houphouet-Boigny went home, Nkrumah was convinced that Houphouet-Boigny was a colonialist agent and Houphouet-Boigny was convinced that Nkrumah was a local imperialist; subsequent relations between their two countries proved each to be correct in his own mind.

Colonel Christophe Soglo and President Hamani Diori, and their followers, exchanged insults during the half year of bad relations between Dahomey and Niger in 1963–64; each called the other "colonialist" and "revolutionary." Further examples could be given in every instance of bad relations between two countries.

Ideology can be used for justification. Even where motivation is unclear, ideology serves to legitimize policy choices and make them more palatable to other states (as well as rendering them more acceptable to the internal audience). The very ambiguity of ideological criteria makes the myths all the more useful. The mechanics of justification are complex.[6] It appears to strengthen the ideological base at least as much and perhaps more than it strengthens the policy; that is, each successive use of a myth enmeshes that myth into the current web of beliefs, yet if a state felt a policy necessary but unjustifiable in ideological terms it would still execute the policy. Algeria's inaction on French atomic explosions and Mali's dependence on Abidjan are cases where "counter-ideological" decisions were made for other, stronger reasons. But such cases appear to be rare. The more states justify a policy for a certain reason, the harder it becomes to break ranks (a point discussed in greater detail below), and states become prisoners of their justifications. However, the ambiguity of the myths and the emergence of new—or differently perceived—situations make escape possible.

Ideology is power. Just as it legitimizes authority and creates solidarity inside states, it also creates solidarity among states and gives international influence to the ideologues. Employed this way, it helps the new African states to overcome their powerlessness by using symbols and values as a more readily available and more rapidly constructed power base than material elements of national power. If power is the ability to produce intended effects, the state which can pose as the Rome, Mecca, or Moscow of the belief-system, and thus which can decree orthodoxy and appeal for solidarity, is in a position of power. Africa still has no shrines and sacred sites, but it does have contending prophets. (Perhaps Addis

[6] Much more research needs to be done on this theoretical problem, probably most helpfully along lines suggested by Clifford Geertz in David Apter (ed.), *Ideology and Discontent* (New York: Free Press of Glencoe, 1964).

Ababa may in time grow into its title of "the capital of Africa," and certainly the commitment of the King of Kings' prestige at both the Addis Ababa summit and the Bamako truce meeting was more influential than would have been the commitment of, say, David Dacko of the Central African Republic or even simply Keita.) Guinea, Ghana, and Algeria all suggest that they have the authority to decree what is truly African conduct. Algeria effectively wielded revolutionary and African unity symbols to gain neutrality or support from other African states in the Algerian-Moroccan border war. By propagating ideas of colonial reparations, coinciding with French feelings of *noblesse oblige* and *mission civilisatrice*, Algeria strengthens its otherwise weak hand in aid negotiations with France.

Ideology also indicates possibilities for action. The matter is delicate. Ideology does not tell what to do in a particular situation, in the sense of how to carry out a policy. Rather, it creates limited options. Guinea had a range of options in foreign policy at the time of its independence—including, at least, an alliance with Liberia, and splendid isolation—but in choosing union with Ghana and a special relationship with the U.S.S.R., it acted in an ideologically natural and approved fashion. This is not to ignore other important factors influencing Guinea's choice, but it does show the influence of myths in affecting policy. When Soudan (now Mali) was left as the only member of the Mali Federation, it would have been more in its interest to join the Entente, assuring an outlet to the sea, a further slap at Senegal, and a reconciliation with its former Rassemblement Démocratique Africain (RDA) partners. But it could not bring itself to do this. Instead, it joined the UAS, where its benefits were slim but its ideological myths untainted; it was only through the initiative of Houphouet-Boigny, who was untrammeled by ideological considerations, that Mali was assured a satisfactory supply port. Even at the loss of several million dollars, Ahmed Ben Bella proclaimed that if, in the seizure of French land, revolutionary socialist morality contravened diplomatic commitments, he "couldn't care less." Tanganyika favored an African army because national armies were considered to be useless except as instruments of divisive Cold War imperialism. When Ghana coveted Togo, it could pursue its policy by insults, claims, threats, and diplomatic pressures, but not by military means, as much because of the "un-African" nature of state use of violence in such a case as for any other reason. Ideology affects policy choices, above all by limiting alternatives.

Even more important is the function of ideology in limiting others' policy choices, a function that combines the two preceding points. Although the current myth maintains that African states wrested independence from the colonial powers by mass action—a good example of the use of ideology to explain events—African leaders in private conversation frequently admit that an important —we would say, the major—factor in independence was the acceptance of the myth of self-determination by both the colonial powers and the African leaders. The colonial pact was broken, and once it was broken—but only then—force could not hold the colonies.[7] Colonialism has become unthinkable. An essential role of ideology is to decree the unthinkable, and thus tie the hands of the enemy with his own inhibitions. Thus, when Ghana claims that its security is endangered by the presence of Belgians and Americans in the Congo, it does not mean that Western troops are going to invade Accra from a base in Leopoldville; it means that any form of colonial return weakens the myth that colonialism is unthinkable, for this myth—and hence the security of Africa—is indivisible. Guinea's *non*-vote in the 1958 referendum made any policy but independence difficult in French West Africa, and the independence of the Mali Federation made it impossible. The notion that ex-colonial states should give aid to their former colonies as reparation for the exactions of past decades that furthered European development is at the same time an ideological explanation of events that makes acceptance of aid compatible with newly independent dignity, a means of strengthening African states' hands in aid negotiations, and an attempt to make the cessation of aid un-

[7] This is a major thesis of Stephane Bernard, *Le Conflit franco-marocain 1943–1956* (Brussels: Institut de sociologie de l'Université libre de Bruxelles, 1963). An extreme statement supporting the opposite view is made by Y. A. Yudin, in Thomas Perry Thornton (ed.), *The Third World in Soviet Perspective* (Princeton, N.J.: Princeton University Press, 1964), p. 254. In a speech to the third National Congress of the Parti Démocratique de la Guinée (PDG), Sékou Touré is equivocal; *The International Policy of the Democratic Party of Guinea*, VII (Conakry: PDG, n.d. [1963]), 21.

thinkable—thus insulating it from the Cold War vagaries and the danger of a Russo-American agreement made without consulting the developing nations. Algeria, Egypt, and Ghana have worked to make the continued presence of colonial troops and the existence of postcolonial defense agreements unthinkable. In North Africa, they have been aided by the Moroccan left and by Tunisia, which shares this view; Libya then became the target of their pressure. In Black Africa, Ghana was helped by the Nigerian opposition, its ideological ally; the Anglo-Nigerian treaty was abrogated, a projected treaty with Sierra Leone was never signed, and British troops were withdrawn from East Africa. It is interesting that Guinea and Mali have not been able to impose this ideological limitation of alternative policies on other former French African states (with the limited exception of Upper Volta). In each case, ideology, by interpreting past events and indicating future dangers, has created international myths that give African states greater power and protection than they could otherwise obtain.

It is in keeping with the nature of ideology that another important function is to outline the new order or political culture toward which foreign policy moves. Because of the assurance function of ideology, this world order is both a goal and a promise. Safe landing on the shores of the promised land depends on correct perception of the direction in which the wave of the future moves; hence, belief in correct explanations of past events and future dangers is necessary for the ideal to be attained. For this reason, foreign policies based on ideology show great activity. The state has a broader task than simply defending its interests; it must not only change its relation to other states or its place in the state system, but also change the system itself. "We are a totally committed state, and ours are revolutionary objectives, aiming at fundamental changes, radical transformations. Accordingly, *our diplomacy must have a militant character, constantly in keeping with the nature of our political commitment*," said Touré.[8] To the ideologue, the external environment must be revised in order to secure domestic goals and support the internal system. This visionary and revisionist aspect also makes plain the total nature of ideology. The new order is not only internal, it is above all external, indivisible, universal. The

---

8 Touré, *op. cit.*, p. 8.

minute it starts to lose these characteristics, it begins to compromise, loses its purity, and weakens its solidarity function.

Here lies the greatest difference between national-interest and ideological policies. The foreign policy based on interest seeks to achieve a place within the state system; it accepts its environment and seeks to fit within it. The ideological policy works to create a new environment because it can find no secure place for itself within the extant state system. *"Our interests, the interests of our people,"* said Touré, *"are subordinate to a new definition of international relations that should respect the personality of each people, the freedom of each nation, the territorial integrity and property of each state."*[9] Algeria and Ghana cannot be secure in an Africa where colonialism still exists, no matter how far away, whereas Gabon and Madagascar have been less concerned by colonies, particularly where distant. Similarly, Ethiopia and Liberia have not always regarded colonial rule in Africa as incompatible with the existence of independent states but merely as a threat to individual state security. Thus, Algeria and Ghana feel they must eradicate colonialism and the exploitation of one state by another from the system of international relations. Less ideologically oriented states feel only that they must eliminate the danger of conquest to their own frontiers.

IV

The picture presented up to this point has been of two contrasting criteria for foreign-policy-making, each slightly overlapping but each representing a basically different and distinct approach to foreign policy. Ideology is idealistic, activist, combative, revisionist, visionary, purist, maladaptive, and deductive; national interest is realistic, modest, constructive, conservative, evaluative, compromising, adaptive, and inductive. Such descriptions, of course, are stereotypes; they are far more clear-cut than reality. Thus far, a somewhat unreal distinction has been maintained between ideologically motivated states and those whose policy is determined by considerations of national interest. In fact, in Africa, all states are revisionist and all share some attachment and suscepti-

[9] *Ibid.*, p. 59.

bility to ideological myths. All Africa bears an antipathy to colonialism as a force and as a system for international relations, even if states vary in their response to it. All Africa accepts the newly independent state as the working unit, whose continuing existence is both the guarantor and the beneficiary of the ideology. Like any state, the new countries of Africa adopt a *status quo* attitude toward what they have and a revisionist attitude toward what they seek.

Instead, ideology and national interest are two extremes of a range of foreign-policy criteria. Between the extremes are three more common but less clear situations: those states that speak ideologically and act according to interest, those states that mix their motives for the same end, and those states that contribute to a sort of situational dialectic in which their ideological policies, confronted by the pressures of reality, produce a new environment that is different from the *status quo ante* but that falls short of the ideal. These way stations on the motivational range are not neat cubbyholes that states occupy with any constancy. A particular state's policy may fit one category at one time and another later on. No complete listing and categorization of all African foreign-policy actions can be made, but characteristic examples can be given.

Purely ideological policies do exist. One group of examples includes the support revolutionary-idealist regimes give to subversion against other African states and territories. In almost all cases, there is no direct state interest involved, particularly where the target states are distant from the agent states. Instead, ideology is used to identify the friend and the enemy, give support to the friend on the basis of an accepted view of the forces of history, and justify the action. Ghana's support of the Sawaba against the Niger Government, of the Union of Cameroon Peoples (UPC) against the Cameroon Government, and of the CNL against the government of the Congo (Leopoldville), resulted from ideological policy decisions, as did Algeria's support for liberation movements in the Portuguese colonies and in Portugal itself.

Another, broader case concerns the ideological phase of African alliances and counteralliances, between late 1960 and early 1963, and the issues on which the various groups based their split. During those years, impelled by the Congo issue (Lumumba vs. Kasa-vubu), the Algerian issue (unconditional war and recognition of the Algerian Provisional Government vs. negotiations), and the lesser Mauritanian issue (presumably precolonial unity vs. succes-sor-state legitimacy), African states channeled their search for unity into a search for ideologically compatible allies. The group founded at Casablanca was the response to the Brazzaville Group and the stimulus to the creation of the Monrovia Group. Although there was not total ideological homogeneity in any of these groups, the split remained as long as the ideological issues lasted. A new and similar split arose under the impact of the new Congo issue. Although no new groups were formed, the revitalization of the Brazzaville Group (Union Africaine et Malgache—UAM) as the Organisation Commune Africaine et Malgache (OCAM), and the Conakry-Bamako meetings of the insurgency supporters, were ideological reactions to the situation. Algerian friendship with Cuba and Ghanaian animosity toward the European Common Market are also ideological choices.

Meetings are also often sponsored for ideological reasons. Ghana's self-identification in ideological terms gave it the role of calling both the Conference of Independent African States and the All-African Peoples Conference in 1958, and Algeria's revisionist view of international relations, coupled with its revolutionary mis-sion to implement that view, led it to host the abortive second Afro-Asian Conference in 1965. The ideological element is clearer in such cases of strong initiative than in more routine cases, such as the site of UAM or Casablanca Group meetings. In a broader sense, Ghana's view of African unity, erected into an ideology, gives it a mission to propose, pressure, reiterate, and experiment in order to foster this policy. Such action is an ideological impera-tive, not a policy serving the interest of one state. Finally in the list of ideological examples, foreign-policy actions have been car-ried out, in response to pressure, in terms of the unthinkable. Ni-geria's cancellation of the Anglo-Nigerian defense pact and Libyan moves under Egyptian pressure to terminate American and British base agreements are such cases. Although the prestige element in the case of meetings may be an exception, ideological policies generally answer the question "Will it help the ideology?" not "Will it help the state?"

National interest has also been invoked in similar situations, although with different resulting policies. Dahomey's hesitation between the Mali Federation and the Entente, action during the Togolese revolt, and sporadic initiatives toward a Benin Union, all closely related to economic needs and political threats, were decided with national interest in mind. Ethiopia's reaction to Somali incursions, the Kenyan-Ethiopian defense pact, and Ethiopian closure of the Haud border—although a policy of debatable wisdom—were designed to defend the national territory. The Moroccan reaction in the Algerian-Moroccan border war was both a defense of the national territory and an attempt to pressure Algeria into settling the problem of territorial limits. Libya's and Liberia's defense pacts with Great Britain and the United States, and the West and Equatorial African Regional Defense Councils with France, also provide for defense of the national territory.

A number of cases of national-interest policy can be drawn from African relations with European countries. Not only do they serve to enhance the economic well-being of the state, but they ignore the ideological rejection of the policy. The broadest example is that of the association of the Eighteen with the European Common Market, but a bilateral relationship such as the Franco-Moroccan agreement, is also a case in point. A particularly pointed example is Tunisia's 1958 agreement to receive the pipeline from Ejele, ending in La Skhirra, a policy to its own economic benefit, despite protests of a break in solidarity from fighting Algeria. A similar case of a national-interest policy, with an African, not a European, state, is the Sudanese-Egyptian Nile agreement of 1959. The Liberian approach to African unity, first developed in conversations with Touré in late 1958, and embodied in parts of the OAU charter, appears to be a good example of a way to approach the problem from a nonideological, national-interest point of view; state sovereignty and territorial integrity are maintained and ways are envisaged to enhance the economic well-being and individual personality of participating members. In sum, policies in the national interest are designed as a response to the question, "Will it help the state?"

However, it is seen that there is much in the current African scene that reinforces the need for at least ideological justification of a policy, even if the decision is made on the basis of other criteria. A striking case was the Algerian-Moroccan war, which was justified in Algeria, not as defense of the national territory, which it was (if it was defense at all), but as defense of the revolution against the backward forces of the Moroccan monarchy, which it was not. The war was simply used by the Algerian solidarity-makers as a means of creating national cohesion, defined in ideological terms. Colonel Soglo acted the same way in Dahomey's quarrel with Niger, perhaps with slightly greater justification. On occasion, the state may adopt a national-interest policy while proclaiming an opposite policy in ideological terms, another way of bridging the ideology–national-interest gap. The policies of Ghana and other states toward the Republic of South Africa are good examples; trade continues, while the tropical African countries continue to call for economic boycotts for ideological reasons. Ghana adopts a similar policy toward foreign aid, balancing its acceptance of financial assistance with vigorous attacks on the neocolonialist donors for their aid policies, a clear case of verbal compensation to preserve dignity compatible with ideological values. Mali acted similarly in accepting transshipment of goods through the Ivory Coast and Upper Volta after the breakup of the Mali Federation, even making the commercial arrangements through the Bamako Chamber of Commerce in order to avoid state involvement. Such actions maximize the advantages of both interest and ideological criteria. Frequently, the pressures of need and the complexity of motivations go beyond the point where the policy can simply be dismissed as two-faced or dishonest, although on occasion the result is to tighten the ideological inhibitions to the point where future actions of the same type in the national interest become impossible. What may once be face-saving justification may later become a prison, at least temporarily. More frequently, the state simply reverses itself or continues to say one thing in order to do another. An example is Nasser's rejection (quickly retracted) of American aid.

A more common way of reconciling ideology and national interest is by mixing motives. When considerations of national interest coincide with the recommendations of ideology, no false justifications or inconsistencies are necessary. It is impossible to separate the two motives in the formation of the Entente. A similar political point of view brought the four states together, but complementary economic interests in sharing the Solidarity Fund and the Abidjan-Niger and Benin-Niger trade routes was of equal importance. Algeria's friendship with the U.S.S.R. is clearly dictated by ideological affinity between regimes that have a common revolutionary experience and have similarities in their world views, but, as long as this relation does not scare away French aid and assistance, it is also in the interest of Algeria to diversify its trade and aid sources. A similar relation with the United States would satisfy only the interest criteria (although it might do it better).

In the end, ideology bows before reality; the state acts in its own interest or it runs the danger of disappearing—or at least its government runs the risk of being overthrown by a counter-elite that places problem-solving before ideology. Ideological policies appear to have given way before policies with a more direct relation to the interests of the state. The UAS has gone; the Entente remains and grows. The Casablanca Group has dissolved; the Brazzaville Group has restored its solidarity and increased its membership. The ideological splits among the seekers of African unity have been replaced by an Organization of African Unity that is compatible with, if not always beneficial to, the interests of the states; the ideologues of unification have been shunted aside. The revolutionary-idealists have twice threatened the national sovereignty of the Congo, and twice failed. Ideological objections to any association with Europe have crumbled, while the ideologically based coalition between the nationalist revolution and the Communist revolution has not (yet!) materialized. Perhaps Africa is only proving the truth, long proclaimed by students of international relations, that a state acts in its own interest, for its own self-preservation, to maximize its own security; other considerations eventually give way.

Whatever the truth in this summation, it is only a caricature. On one hand, it has been seen that ideology has a role to play and a need to fulfill; like national interest, it is a response to reality, and especially to the reality of frustration and insecurity that characterize the place of African states in the present state system. This situation is likely to continue. In fact, it is likely that the search for ideology will intensify, and that ideology will continue to hold an important place in the perception of the states' national interests. Africans are a long way from accepting the reality of their situation, the revolutionary-idealists being furthest away. If, as present trends and conditions indicate, rising expectations will not be satisfied, reality will become less, not more, acceptable and ideology will become more necessary (in the minds of the Africans). Furthermore, if present ideologies are incapable of explaining, ordering, and prescribing satisfactorily—that is, if they lose almost all touch with reality—they will only contribute to the increase of dissatisfaction, rejection, and likelihood of revolution. In such a case, for both incumbent and opposition ideologues, there is pressure to resort to means of violence and coercion to keep their following, something that is not necessary if the ideology is satisfying and thus voluntarily accepted; foreign scapegoats and external distractions are foreign policy corollaries that have frequently been used at such times.

On the other hand, out of the confrontation of ideology and national interest, the victory of realism has not been clear cut, even if the new order assured by ideology has not been attained. The collapse of the Casablanca Group did not lead to the reemergence of unity on the colonial pattern, but to a universal African organization which can serve as a framework and even on occasion as a problem-solving institution in a mobile African subsystem. Commonly, if not universally, a whole series of actions and conditions are regarded as unthinkable (at least for the present): not only colonial rule and legal inequality of states, but also colonial land ownership, postcolonial military bases, direct Cold War alliances, extra-African military intervention, termination of foreign aid, unaltered commercial bilateralism, etc. States may return to close cooperation with the former metropole, but they do so with a new mentality, with complexes replaced by a sense of dignity. The process of creating a new political culture for the state system is slow, but so is the process of creating awareness and developing perception of national interests. The process of using ideology as power until the substantive elements of national power can be built up, and the process of decreeing equality on the basis of ideological rationalizations until states that are equal in sovereignty become more nearly equal in power, are both inventive responses to the powerlessness of new states. When aspirations and reality at least come in sight of each other, when means become commensurate with state ends, when African states find that they can defend their interests within an extant state system— in sum, when the frustrations induced by insecurity reach a more "normal" level, where they can be lived with—then, African decision-makers can think more in terms of their interests and less in terms of idealist, revisionist ideologies.[10] Obviously, Africa is not yet at this point.

[10] In addition to references cited, particularly useful material has been found in Karl Mannheim, *Ideology and Utopia* (New York: Harcourt, Brace, 1952); William Friedland and Carl G. Rosberg, Jr. (eds.), *African Socialism* (Stanford, Calif.: Stanford University Press, 1964); Leonard Binder, *The Ideological Revolution in the Middle East* (New York: Wiley, 1964); John H. Kautsky, *Political Change in Underdeveloped Countries* (New York: Wiley, 1962); Carl J. Friedrich (ed.), *The Public Interest* (New York: Atherton Press, 1962); and Pierre Bonnafe and Michel Carty, "Les Idéologies politiques en pays en voie de développement," *Révue française de science politique*, June, 1962, 417–25. Some of the arguments in the present discussion on national interest have come from the author's *International Relations in the New Africa* (Englewood Cliffs, N.J.: Prentice-Hall, 1966).

III

Economic Determinants

ANDREW M. KAMARCK

The economic forces at work and the economic structure of a country are important factors in both its domestic politics and its foreign policy. Very simply, to survive you must eat. The way in which an individual or nation has to act to get food and the other desired commodities is bound to affect nearly everything it does. The extent to which economics actually influences the domestic or foreign policy of a country cannot, however, be as easily explained as some Marxists or other economic determinists believe. These policies depend on the strength of the economic forces at work, on the awareness of the economic factors by the government leaders and the other leading elements of the country, and on the strength of the other forces involved, e.g., nationalism and cultural objectives. In some cases, economic considerations may be the overriding factor, as seems to be true in Malawi's refusal to take drastic action against Portuguese Africa. Even though Dr. Banda's commitment to African solidarity and to African independence is strong, the economic factor was stated clearly and succinctly in his reported remark "No country can reasonably be expected to cut its own throat."

In most cases, however, the economic factor is not as paramount; it may not be as well appreciated or other factors may be given more weight. The overriding of economic considerations was clearly seen, for example, in the Moroccan Government's insist-

55

ence on the removal of U.S. air bases from Moroccan soil even though they provided a considerable income to Morocco and employed thousands of Moroccans. In addition, the air bases undoubtedly gave the United States a special interest in giving Morocco a priority in economic aid. However, these considerations may have influenced the deliberate pace at which the bases were phased out.

The economic forces affecting politics and foreign policy stem from (a) the structure and nature of a country's domestic economy and its external economic and financial relationships; (b) the objectives of the government and people as to the kind of economy and external economic relationships they want; and (c) the tension between the first and second of these, that is, the tension between "what is" and "what ought to be" or "what is desired to be." The last two points, people being people, are at least as important as the actual economic forces in operation.

The Impact of the Structure of the Economy

The African countries are highly dependent economies. That is, they are dependent on the outside world. This statement requires some modification. The African economies are really dualistic, i.e., one part is still the same age-old subsistence economy: people growing their own food, building their own houses, and carrying water in the gourds they have grown themselves. The other part, the money or market economy, is the modern, the dynamic part of economic life: it is growing cotton or coffee for the market; buying radios, bicycles, textiles at the village store; it is traveling hundreds of miles by truck or train to find work in a factory or mine. And, it is this market economy—the economy of the future—which is dependent on the outside world.

On the average, a quarter of the market output of an African country is sold abroad and a larger fraction of its money purchases comes from abroad. Africa is still at that stage of development and in that process of development where the main engine of economic growth has been, and still is, the growth of export earnings. Consequently, the situation tends to be that the richer the country, the higher the relative per capita importance of its foreign trade. The richer the country, the more it depends on the

outside world for continuation of its existing economy and for
further economic growth. South Africa is becoming the one exception to this, simply because in its development, South Africa
has passed beyond this earlier stage and has now reached the in-
dustrializing stage. In South Africa, at present, the growth of the
economy depends more on the development of the internal market for manufactures than on the growth of exports to the rest of
the world.

The other African countries continue, in the main, to be dependent also on the import of capital and of key trained people
for the growth of their economies. The African countries, on the
average, receive a relatively greater flow of capital from abroad
than countries in other parts of the world. With only a few exceptions, the African countries receive more than $3 per capita of
capital annually from abroad. Algeria and Swaziland actually received more than $25 per capita of capital imports in 1963. In the
rest of the world, the developing countries have been receiving on
the average rather less than $3 per capita. In many African coun-
tries, almost all of the recorded investment is financed from
abroad. In most, the size and the pace of the inflow of investment
funds may make the difference between a rapid growth of the
economy, as in the Ivory Coast for instance, with a 10 per cent or
more growth in the last few years, or a very slow growth or near-
stagnancy. In this, again, South Africa is an exception since it is
now practically independent of inflows of capital from abroad.

The economic health and economic future of the African countries thus is heavily influenced by their foreign economic and political relationships. But while the rest of the world is vital
economically for the African countries, African trade and investments are comparatively of little importance to the rest of the
world. For the United States, trade with Africa and American investments in Africa represent under 5 per cent of the world total
of American trade and investments. For West European countries,
African trade and investments are more important but, aside from
France, trade with the African countries is under 10 per cent of
their total trade while investments are minimal or nonexistent.
Even for France, the trade with Africa is under one-fifth of her
total and the percentage has been shrinking over the last twenty

years. The loss of this trade would be far from having a disastrous impact on Europe. The example of the Netherlands, which has grown in prosperity since its loss of the Dutch East Indies, shows how even a much greater impact can be taken in stride by an industrialized country at the present time. Even if the African countries were organized in a monolithic bloc, they could not use economic power as a bludgeon to serve their political interests in the world arena. They just do not have enough economic strength. They are rather in the position where it makes more economic sense to consider using their foreign political relations, for example, their votes and influence in the U.N., to serve their economic ends.

The foregoing in a sense has overstated the case because the facts are that, today, in the modern world economy, it is difficult to argue that any one nation, including the United States, has or can have decisive economic influence on the rest of the world. Even the United States could not successfully wield its enormous economic power alone to force another country into a policy, when the other country felt strongly enough to resist. Even in the case of Cuba, which was economically closely tied to the United States, economic action by the United States to secure changes in the Cuban Government has not been spectacularly successful. The world today is closer together economically and, at the same time, the degree of economic control that any one nation has over others is quite small. Certainly, no developing nation or group of developing nations can feel that it can exercise decisive international economic power.

Since World War II, the growth of the international economic and financial organizations is resulting more and more in international economic and financial decisions being determined by negotiations rather than being imposed by any one or group of nations. To an increasing extent, decisions affecting the international economy, and thus the national economies, are being made through the international economic and financial institutions, i.e., through organizations such as the World Bank, the International Monetary Fund, GATT, and the new U.N. Trade and Development Board. In these instances, no one country is dominant and decisions are reached more by consensus than by vote. And, in these institutions, the African states are able to exercise their legitimate influence and get a hearing of their needs and aspirations.

In this kind of international economic context, the world today is quite different from that of the 1930's. Then, the growth of bilateralism forced many small countries into separate face-to-face bargaining sessions with a country with much greater economic power. It is not surprising that many small countries then fell into the economic clutches of an economically dominant great power. Today, in a world that is based on multilateral trade and convertible currencies (except for some remnants of bilateralism mostly preserved by the Soviet countries), a small country usually has a multiplicity of markets and suppliers to choose from. It can make its choices on the basis of what is most economically advantageous to it in each individual transaction. It is true that developing countries, which usually produce only a few commodities, and primary products at that, do not have the flexibility and possibilities of the developed countries, but the present situation is still an immense improvement over the prewar world.

In operating in the present international economic and financial context, the African countries have several choices. The economic ends they strive to achieve are usually to secure the best paying markets, stable remunerative prices for their exports, and the most generous provision of economic aid and technical assistance. To achieve these economic objectives, in some cases but not all, an African country has an option to build close relations with a particular donor country or group and hope that by loyal cooperation it will get optimum benefit. Or a country may decide to try to maneuver among the various donor countries, perhaps try to play off one against the other and so attempt to maximize the favorable treatment and aid that it may get. A third possibility is simply to play the multilateral game and hope that the country will not suffer. Most of the French-speaking countries have chosen (they essentially were not offered any other comparably generous alternative) to work closely with France. From the *economic* point of view, it is hard to argue that they have been wrong, since the French economic and financial aid to the countries that have remained closely linked with France and the European Common Market has been so generous that it is scarcely possible that another course of action could have produced better economic results.

The two countries that did not follow this pattern, Guinea and Mali, in recent years have been re-establishing their relationships with France. Mali, in fact, remained an associate member of the European Common Market and never destroyed all her links with the franc zone.

The non-French-speaking African countries did not have available to them from other Western powers the same comparatively generous treatment that France provided to its former colonies, and most of the African countries have been quick to learn that close ties with the Sino-Soviet countries were not a substitute for trade and aid from the rest of the world. Playing the field successfully, that is, playing aid givers against one another, requires a large cadre of diplomatic and financial negotiators that probably only two or three countries in Africa possess. In general, the African countries, in most cases from choice, have made no attempt to use political maneuvering as a technique of securing aid, but have remained politically true to themselves and played the multilateral economic game of granting no particular favors to anyone. Tunisia has probably been the most successful in securing aid from a whole range of sources, both Western and Eastern, while at the same time removing the vestiges of her former dependent status and becoming no country's client. Ghana, thus far, has been much less successful, but has been able to secure help from both the East and West.

As exporters of primary products, the African countries have a common cause with developing countries elsewhere in the world, i.e., to try to secure cooperative international action toward control of the market for their products in order to get and maintain favorable prices and to minimize fluctuations. However, in many cases, as the most dynamic and lowest-cost producers in many primary commodities, frequently their economic interest is to try to get a larger share of the market away from producers in Asia or Latin America. In this way, they may have an opportunity to secure faster economic growth than is permitted by the general sluggish growth in demand for most of the commodities they produce. Consequently, in negotiating international commodity agreements, the intelligent course for the African countries, except in cases where they already dominate the market as in cocoa, may be to remain outside the agreement as long as possible in order to take advantage of the price umbrella created and maintained by the other producers. Once they are within the agreement, their interest may be to secure flexibility in quotas so that it will be possible for them to get, in time, a growing share of the market. Finally, their interests may be served by having the price set at a level that will not encourage high-cost producers, elsewhere, to stay in production or to go into production. Again, their interest may be to keep prices from getting too high to prevent the encouragement of production of substitutes elsewhere in the world. These interests of the Africans, of course, may in very specific cases put them into direct conflict with producers elsewhere in the world.

Along the same lines, the eighteen African associate members of the European Common Market, with free entry for their products into the Common Market, have a direct interest in trying to preserve this rapidly growing market for themselves, against the Asian, Latin American, and other African producers of the same products. Again, in this way, the countries involved would be able to secure a more rapid growth of their exports and, therefore, of their economies than if they had to gear their production to the slow overall growth of the total world consumption of primary products. The other African producers have two choices in this situation. One is to try to join with the Latin American and Asian producers to persuade the European Common Market to eliminate or to reduce the preferences given to associate members. The other alternative is to attempt to have the preferences extended to their products as well. It is also possible to try to operate on both fronts simultaneously. Nigeria and the East African countries, which are among the most affected outsiders, have been negotiating with the European Common Market to secure an agreement that will allow entry into the Common Market of their products on some basis of equality with the African associate members. The three Maghrib countries have also intermittently tried to work out an acceptable relationship with the Common Market. It is not at all surprising, consequently, that these African countries appoint some of their ablest economic negotiators to be their diplomatic representatives in Brussels.

The bulk of African trade now is with Western Europe. North America is a very poor second except in the case of a few countries, notably Liberia and Ethiopia. Exports of some of the coffee producers (Uganda, Angola) to the United States are becoming important. The Soviet bloc is a very poor third, but the biggest potential unexploited market for the African primary producers is the Soviet group of countries. These countries, in relation to the per capita income levels they have reached, consume only a fraction of the coffee, cocoa, palm oil, and other products that Western countries consume. If the Soviet bloc bought tropical products in relation to per capita income on the same scale as the Western Europeans or the Americans, the African producers would have a market for another $2 or $3 billion of African export items, and the African standard of living could rise by around 50 per cent. This "import gap" has many implications for African-Soviet relations and for the international relations of Africa generally. Both the Africans and the Soviet Union are becoming conscious of this "gap." One indication of this was the announcement by the Soviet Union at the end of 1964 that it was going to abolish customs duties on tropical products. This decision at present, of course, is meaningless since, in the Soviet centralized economy, the decision to buy or not to buy African products is not influenced by the existence of customs duties, but is a bureaucratic decision. Since it is the government foreign-trade monopoly that buys a product abroad, the fact that a customs duty may be levied on it when the product is passed on to a government sales organization has no influence on the foreign-trade monopoly's original decision. This Sino-Soviet foreign-trade structure has had some foreign-policy repercussions in Africa, however: It makes good business sense to the foreign-trade monopoly to barter Soviet machinery for African products which are easily salable elsewhere for foreign exchange, which is not the case with the machinery. Both the U.A.R. and Ghana have discovered that cotton or cocoa sold to the Soviet bloc against purchases of Soviet goods has wound up for sale in Western Europe. The U.A.R. and Ghana have thus found themselves in competition with their own products. However, if the Soviet Union evolves toward a more decentralized economy with buying decisions determined more and more by price and by the consumers themselves (and there are some indications that this is taking place), the elimination of the customs duties would help in the growth of African exports to Eastern Europe. If so, the opening of this large market could provide an important propulsive force to the African economies for the next one or two decades.

At present, for a considerable period, there is little potential for the growth of Chinese-African trade on an economic basis. The kind of products that China itself is trying to export abroad, i.e., simple manufactures, is in fact the type of products that the African countries in the not too distant future will themselves be hoping to export. The standard of living in China is, at present, and for a long time to come, too low to provide much of a market for present African exports—and China is likely to keep them out to save foreign exchange for purchase of machinery. The purchase by China, from time to time, of raw cotton or tea can only be a temporary phenomenon resulting from a crop failure or an *ad hoc* political decision in China. The Africans are also likely, of course, to find themselves in competition with other developing countries, e.g., India or Pakistan, in the field of simple manufactured products.

INTRA-AFRICAN ECONOMIC RELATIONS

While the most important economic relations of the African states are with states outside Africa, there are, in the case of some African states, also important economic relationships with other African states. For the land-locked African state, the dependence on one or another African state for a way to the sea can be a dominant factor in its diplomatic as well as economic relations with its neighbor. For a country like Malawi that has no choice but to use routes through Mozambique to the sea, good relations with Mozambique are vital, as Dr. Banda has indicated. Countries such as Zambia, Uganda, Rwanda, Burundi, the Central African Republic, Chad, Niger, Mali, and Upper Volta that have two or more feasible routes to the sea may be in a somewhat more flexible position. The degree of flexibility may be severely curtailed, however, because of the cost of shifting trade from one route to another. The size of the cost may be a determining factor in the foreign relations of the country. Where traffic is such that it must be carried by rail, road transport may be almost prohibitive, and the cost and time to build an alternative railway may rule this out as a real possibility.

Another important economic relationship among African countries stems from the movement of labor. For Basutoland, Swaziland, Bechuanaland, and Malawi, the employment opportunities in South Africa are very important if not vital. "African leaders in the three High Commission Territories and in Malawi have stated that they could not support economic measures [against South Africa] because of their dependence on trade with the Republic and on earnings from migrant labor employed in South Africa"[1] (whose need for this labor is considerably less acute).

The need for their people to have the opportunity to continue to be able to work in another country is also an important economic factor for countries such as Rwanda vis-à-vis Uganda, Niger and Chad vis-à-vis the Sudan, Niger and Upper Volta vis-à-vis Ghana and the Ivory Coast, and Dahomey vis-à-vis most of the former French West African countries. The country providing employment also is interested economically in seeing that the labor continues to come in. In most cases, however, the need for continued opportunity to get jobs is more important for the "proletarian" country than is the need for the "employer" country to import labor.

The potential for industrialization in most of Africa is greatly dependent on the extent to which other African countries allow African products to enter their markets. Aside from Nigeria, and to some extent Algeria, the Democratic Republic of the Congo (Leopoldville), and South Africa, none of the African countries have, or are likely to have in the immediate future, large enough markets to allow much industrialization to get started. Only if several countries get together in a customs union or a free-trade

[1] W. A. Hance, "Efforts to Alter the Future: Economic Action," in Amelia C. Leiss (ed.), *Apartheid and the United Nations* (New York: Carnegie Endowment for International Peace, 1965), p. 102.

area to pool their purchasing power by creating a single market will it be possible for industrialization to get a good start in most of Africa in the next generation. This should be an important economic force toward unity if it is fully appreciated.

A common market, however, is not an unmixed blessing for all its participants. Competition from another African country may prevent the establishment of some industries in a particular country. That is to say, if Country A participates in a common market it may find that even though the common market makes possible the establishment of much more industry than would have been possible before, all of this new industry, plus the few small industries that would in any case have been possible in Country A itself, may be established elsewhere in the common market, i.e., in Country B. This potential loss of industry by Country A may induce it to be against the establishment of a common market or induce it to break up an existing common market, if the matter is not carefully negotiated. In fact, it was this problem that threatened the existence of the East African common market and almost led to its breakup in 1964. Tanganyika felt that all the new industry was being established in Nairobi, Kenya; industry that would otherwise have come to Tanganyika went to Nairobi since it could supply Tanganyika from there without passing tariff barriers because of the common market. It was necessary to try to hold the common market together by the Kampala agreement of May, 1964, which allocated certain industries to Tanganyika.

The problem of the location of an industry also may have important political implications. There is, for example, the question whether the slaughterhouses handling cattle from the Republic of Niger, which are destined for the market in Nigeria, should be located in Niger or Nigeria. As there may be very little economic difference between the two solutions, the decision will depend on negotiations between the two countries.

Economic aid may also be a factor in the political relationships among African states. The financial help that the Ivory Coast makes available to other states (Upper Volta, Niger, and Dahomey) through the Conseil de l'Entente may well help the Ivory Coast take the leadership among these states.

The location of natural resources that are or might be economically important may also become a factor. In those areas where the frontier may be in dispute, or where there are irredendist claims, an agreed solution may be made much more difficult if rich natural resources are also involved. The belief that there might be oil in the northeast corner of Kenya reinforces Kenya's reluctance to consider concession of this area to Somalia. The discovery of oil in the Sahara made both Moroccan and Tunisian claims to parts of the area more important.

THE COLONIAL ECONOMIC STRUCTURE

Some of the new African countries inherited what might be called a "colonial" economic structure. In most of them, much of this had already been changed even prior to independence. In some, however, the Africans found that as unskilled labor they were facing big foreign mining or plantation concerns which were the main buyers of their labor. In some countries, the Africans as peasant producers found themselves confronting a small group of exporting and processing firms which were monopolistic buyers of their crops. (In most countries, however, the colonial governments themselves, after World War II, had set up marketing boards and *caisses de stabilisation* to control the marketing process.) Finally, in their role as consumers of imported commodities, the Africans in some cases had to face the same group of import-export firms which were the main sellers or distributors of the imported commodities. In many countries, there had arisen a class of middlemen between the big European firms and the economically less-developed indigenous population. The role of middlemen was taken by Asians in East Africa and by Levantines and "Coast Africans" in West Africa. To the extent that these factors applied to the structure of an economy, they had a considerable impact on the international politics and foreign policy of the independent African countries. Internally, many of the African governments have tried to set up a "countervailing power" to the strategic power of the big concerns by encouraging the growth of labor unions or government controls or in some cases by nationalizing the concerns. In particular, when the action taken at home in this regard has not been well controlled, disputes have occurred with the developed countries whose citizens or companies are involved. The presence of large elements of foreign origin—e.g., Europeans, Indians, Pakistanis, Lebanese, or Syrians—in key positions of the economy may at times affect the relationships between the host country and the country of origin of the nonindigenous people.

Tension Between Expectations and Reality

Finally, there is the enormous impact of the revolution of rising expectations. A tremendous, largely invisible but important change is going on in Africa: the development throughout the continent of the monetary economy. The impact of education on the youth, of the transistor radio, the movies, and television, and the experience of migrant laborers are enormously building up wants among the people. Everything and everybody are influenced, whether this is immediately evident or not, and the rate at which people are being changed is accelerating. The modern economy with its amazing power to create wealth, to bring about control of disease, to provide means to secure commodities, is having an impact on Africans throughout the continent. The traditional outlook, with the previously accepted passive attitude toward life, is suddenly seen as irrelevant. People now realize they are poor and that something can be done about it; ill health and premature death are seen as avoidable; irksome and unprogressive tribal discipline is seen as the futile worship of impotent gods. The new governments are very much aware of these growing demands and of the new attitude that the world can be changed, but governments are also very much aware of their feeling of helplessness in trying to get something achieved quickly.

Before independence, resentment of the high standard of living of the European officials was an expression of the general resentment against colonialism. After independence, the first generation of the governing elite has inherited the benefits of the positions formerly held by the Europeans. But a larger and larger number of people feel that they should qualify as members of the elite. And even those who may not feel qualified want the benefits of modern life. But the economic reality is that the new economies

cannot afford at this time to spread the standard of living of the
elite to the masses. In some cases, the real question is whether they
can afford it even for the elite, and still get the necessary savings
and investment for the economy to grow. On the one hand, the
benefits could be used as an incentive to call forth extra effort by
people to work to get the rewards; on the other hand, the high
consumption of the elite may hold down the amount of savings
the country generates. (The wrong lesson may be drawn by the
people outside the favored group and that is that the rewards are
to be won not by economic effort but by political effort.)

In brief, the modern elites are faced with a great demand for the
benefits of the Western economy but with a people not yet conscious of the costs that must be paid to get an economy that can
produce those benefits. People acquire new wants and aspirations
much more rapidly than earning capacity can be increased. As Hla
Myint has pointed out, individuals begin to desire "the American
way of life"; on the national level, they desire the latest model of
social security schemes as in the British welfare state. He comments: "It would . . . be a crowning point of irony if some backward countries were to turn towards Communism through an
excessive fondness for the American and British ways of life."[2]

In any case, it is not at all surprising that African leaders turn to
the developed countries for sympathy and help in their predica-
ment and that the pressures upon them and the impatience that it
engenders easily become the dominant factors in their relations
with the rest of the world.

[2] Hla Myint, "An Interpretation of Economic Backwardness," in A. N.
Agarwala and S. P. Singh (eds.), *The Economics of Underdevelopment*
(New York: Oxford University Press, 1963), pp. 93–132.

IV

Military Influences

WILLIAM J. FOLTZ

Military requirements and military techniques have always influenced foreign policy. The show of force, saber and missile rattling, the border incident, and direct invasion are familiar techniques by which nations try to influence the behavior of others. Less dramatically, the nonaggression or mutual defense pact, the acceptance or imposition of foreign military advisers or matériel, and even the disarmament conference are examples of military considerations influencing over-all political aims. By its very existence, a military establishment may influence at least some elements of foreign policy; the military may constitute a powerful pressure group meeting special political or economic goals, or may want a chance to try out its skills on a neighbor. Military matériel and strategic requirements or preferences may also impose special alliances or *rapprochements* other than would normally be desirable. Finally, military weakness may decisively limit the flexibility and credibility of other foreign-policy instruments.

AFRICAN MILITARY ESTABLISHMENTS

Although all African armies are weak by international standards, they vary considerably in size, military effectiveness, and political influence. The greatest differences are between the armies of North Africa (together with Ethiopia and the Sudan) and those of tropical Africa below the Sahara.[1] The armies of North Africa are comparatively large, both in numbers and in terms of money spent on them. Egypt has some 110,000 men under arms and Algeria about 60,000. About 0.44 per cent of North Africa's population is in the regular military (about the same as in Latin America), and the five Arab North African states together spend substantially more on the military than do all the tropical African nations put together. By comparison, only 0.07 per cent of the population of tropical Africa is in the regular military, by far the lowest of any major geographical area, and the most impressive military forces, those of Ghana and Nigeria, each number slightly over 10,000. Small as all these establishments are in absolute terms, it is not uncommon for an African state to spend between 10 and 20 per cent of its budget, and 2 to 5 per cent of its gross national product, on the military, and also to devote a substantial proportion of the foreign aid it receives to military purposes.

African armed forces are almost entirely infantry, with the battalion or perhaps brigade as the basic level of organization. Smaller units of paratroopers or other elite forces may be attached to the regular infantry, and most states have some sort of air force and coast guard with limited surveillance and transport capabilities. Only Egypt has serious air and naval combat forces. Most African states also have some sort of armed gendarmerie or presidential guard which can serve as a domestic aid for the military, or perhaps also as a political and tactical counterweight. Relations are seldom good between these armed police units and the regular army, and most politicians prefer to keep it that way.

With a few local exceptions, the people of Africa seem to regard the military as a respectable if not particularly exalted career, and recruitment to the ranks is seldom a problem, although achieving a politically desirable ethnic balance may be a problem in some countries. Recruiting an officer corps poses more problems. Most of the senior commissioned ranks are usually filled by men who served, often as NCO's, in the former colonial army. Additional recruiting is often handicapped by the dearth of educated men that plagues all sectors of society, and by the relatively more at-

[1] Except where specifically mentioned, the countries in Southern Africa under white rule are not included in the discussion.

tractive, or at least less arduous, careers open to educated men in civilian society. The same is generally the case with noncommissioned technicians and specialists of various sorts, and most African armies, unlike their Latin American counterparts, are short of both officers and specialists. The situation is not as serious in North Africa, where the armies have been able to recruit officers out of a nascent middle class, but even there the lack of reliable and technically trained men limits the rate of military growth in the near future and imperils the armies' discipline and effectiveness at present.

Modern warfare in tropical areas is expensive, requires substantial amounts of complex equipment and spare parts, and above all is a logistical nightmare. The different tropical terrains within a single country—rain forest and savanna, or mountains and desert, for instance—require different equipment, training, and tactics. There are so many limitations on African armies' effectiveness in battle, not just because of the monetary cost, but because African states as a whole are deficient in the technical and organizational skills required to operate and maintain complex machinery and to move large quantities of men and matériel. This lack of skills will take a long time to remedy, even in a relatively up-to-date army such as that of Egypt.

Logistics is a particularly vexing problem, and only Ghana, among Black African states, and Egypt, in North Africa, have shown much ability to move forces about effectively outside their own borders.[2] Roads are bad and often stop at the border, while air or sea transport is expensive and generally dependent on foreigners for operation and maintenance. More than once since 1960, armed clashes over border issues have not materialized because one or both armies could not get to the point of dispute. Logistical difficulties and rough terrain severely curtail the aggressive capabilities of African armies and give the defense a decided advantage. A carefully planned attack of short duration on a neighboring state is about the extent of the large-scale offensive capabilities of

[2] The Ghanaian battalion was virtually the only one to arrive in the Congo with adequate logistic provision. Much of the transport of men and supplies was carried out by the Black Star Line and by Ghana Airways. A regular military post-office and home-rotation system were quickly set up.

any Black African army at the present time. The North African armies, particularly those of Egypt and Algeria, could do quite a bit better, though logistics, particularly for an attacker, would still be a formidable problem.

Whatever attack or defensive potential it may display, the primary duty of an African army is to maintain internal security. In North Africa, this is certainly within the military's capability, but in Black Africa, it is much less certain that an army could put down widespread, organized insurrection without outside help.[3] In times of significant international tension within Africa, internal security duties are likely to become particularly important, and few regimes will feel they can risk sending a major portion of their small military forces abroad for an extended period of time. In this way too, the small size of Africa's armed forces is a decided limitation on the international role they may play.

However limited may be the armaments and however imperfect the organization and techniques they command, the officer corps of most African armies have a strong sense of belonging to a distinct professional calling.[4] This professional identity may be the most important of Europe's legacies to the African officer corps, and is noticeable in even so ineffective an army as the Armée Nationale Congolaise. This professionalism has tended to reinforce officers' pride in their organization and their own technical skills and has led them to oppose political meddling in army affairs. In a more general sense, it has directed their loyalty to the national state, over and above the individuals leading that state, and it has heightened their concern for the state's integrity and safety. In international affairs, like professional soldiers elsewhere in the world, African officers tend to be nationalist, nonideological, and opposed to international military or political adventuring that might weaken the army or otherwise imperil the state. In this sense, at least, they

[3] To put this in crude quantitative terms, there is approximately one North African soldier for every thirty-two adult male civilians and for every 9 square miles of territory. In Black Africa, there are ten times as many civilian men per soldier, and each soldier has, figuratively, 50 square miles to guard.

[4] See the discussion of military professionalism in Samuel P. Huntington, *The Soldier and the State* (Cambridge, Mass.: Harvard University Press, 1957), pp. 7–18, 59–79.

are frequently more conservative than the regimes they serve. These professional characteristics are likely to be strongest where the army has a preindependence tradition of a colonial army on which to rely, or where European training and influence remain strong. It is likely to be weakest where the army has been created *de novo* under unstable conditions after independence, and where it is penetrated and dominated by explicitly political groups. The professional characteristics of the officer corps may be substantially weakened over time in the more ideologically conscious countries if the army is made an active arm of the party (as in Algeria, where the army bore the sobriquet of *le parti armé*), if political considerations dominate officer selection and promotion, or if the civil-military distinction is otherwise destroyed. Tensions of this sort already exist in Mali, Guinea, and Tanzania, and in Algeria have already led the military to oust part of the civilian regime.

The Military as a Political Group

Neither professionalism nor operational weakness means that the military may not play a political role, or even seek to take over some or all of the governmental functions. African armies do have a clear advantage (if not a monopoly) in the control and utilization of recognized instruments of violence within their own countries, and the world has provided enough precedents of military coups to remind political leaders how costly it may be to infuriate the military consistently. Furthermore, the military's usual explicit role of "protecting and defending the constitution and the integrity of the nation" gives it some formal justification for taking an interest in civil affairs. The extreme case is the military *coup d'état* which has taken quite different forms in Africa. In one form, classically illustrated by Egypt, a large army with an educated and homogeneous officer corps, and with some prestige for having played a role in achieving independence, ousts a venal regime which has severely interfered with and humiliated the army, and then takes over all government functions. In another form, a much smaller and less experienced officer corps pushes the army to intervene where a discredited government is unable to maintain public order. The army then aids some civilian group, like labor union leaders or disaffected politicians, to form a government while the army slowly fades into the background. The Congo (Brazzaville) and Dahomey coups are of this pattern. Other coups, such as those of Colonel Joseph Mobutu in the Congo (Leopoldville) and Colonel Houari Boumedienne in Algeria fall somewhere in between.

Aside from such dramatic examples, African military establishments have on the whole exercised surprisingly little of their potential influence on national policy, whether foreign or domestic, particularly if one compares them with their counterparts in Southeast Asia, the Middle East, or Latin America. For example, whereas most Latin American civilian regimes give at least one, and sometimes several cabinet portfolios to military men, it is rare to find even the Ministry of Defense allocated to a member of the military in an African state. Similarly, it is rare to hear of African military leaders consulted by the civil authorities on any but military problems interpreted in the narrowest sense. In Black Africa, where a national leadership crisis as in Senegal or Nigeria, or a breakdown as in Dahomey or Congo (Brazzaville), has brought the African officers to play a political role, their willingness to avoid overt political power or to relinquish it at an early moment has been noteworthy.

This political reluctance derives as much from the strengths of the political order as from the weakness of the military. In most African countries, the regime has considerable prestige and represents a more or less homogeneous elite with fairly compatible ideals and interests. Above all, it is usually the politician, not the soldier, that brought independence and that profits from the revolutionary aura. Whoever the leader of the national military establishment may be, he is certain not to match the president or party leader in personal prestige and charisma. Frequently, the political demands of the preindependence nationalist period obliged the party to organize widely throughout society, to find ways of including or silencing a wide variety of social groups, and to enforce some form of discipline over its members and most politically relevant sectors of society. The military, on the contrary, is formally the creation and servant of the state. It is usually physically or morally separate from society and is commanded by people who were inactive in the independence struggle, either because they were in the colonial army or because they were too young to play a leading role. The African army may be the guardian of the state, but in many countries the party comes close to being the state. This revolutionary aura and elite solidarity is sure to diminish over time, perhaps before the political process has become firmly established. As the older national heroes fall out of favor or die off, other groups and interests in society may take an increasing part in the political process, and the military, if only because it is a disciplined organization, is likely to be one of them. The rash of military coups in December, 1965, and January, 1966, occurred precisely in those countries where disputes or corruption among the civilian political leaders had paralyzed government business and caused substantial disaffection among the people.

Whatever the limits on its formal political power, the military, whether as individuals or as one or more cohesive bargaining groups, can frequently exercise some pressure on the government over issues of direct professional concern. Where the military is an important prop for the regime, as in the Congo (Leopoldville), or where its prestige rivals that of the party, as in Algeria, its influence over some issues may be very great indeed. Most of these issues concern domestic politics, particularly the allocation of budgetary expenditures, but in a few broad areas of foreign policy the African military has exercised a generally conservative influence. Like professional soldiers in many other areas of the world, African military leaders have discouraged wild talk of military adventure against neighboring states. It is the politicians who rattle sabers in Africa, not the soldiers. In their speeches, African generals vow to preserve the state against aggression, not to lead crusades. Partly, this results from the professional military man's aversion to unnecessary war and to loose talk about his area of specialization. Partly, this also results from the African soldier's awareness of how weak an attack force his army really is, and how great is the advantage to the defense in Africa today.

The military's professional sense is likely also to reduce its sympathy for various forms of subversive adventuring in neighboring countries. In Mali, for example, the cooperation that the military gave the civil authorities in training exiles for operations against Senegal, after the breakup of the Mali Federation, was half-hearted at best. To the military, such subversive operations are likely to appear as ineffectual, amateurish efforts that may require the military to go in and pull other people's chestnuts out of the fire once the going gets rough. The military may be more co-operative where the training involves distant countries, since the military danger for the country providing aid is much less. Even in ideologically mobilized states, where the army is under direct party control, the military is likely to restrain radical groups of the *Jeunesse* or Workers Brigade variety that are entrusted to its care. To the degree that the army can constrict their activities or exercise a conservative influence over them, these potentially radical groups may exercise a less upsetting influence in the choice of foreign policy goals by the regime in power.

It is in relations with the major powers that the military is likely to exercise most fully its conservative bias. Almost all senior officers in newly independent states were trained in the former metropolitan country; many, particularly in French-speaking Africa, had extensive service in the colonial armies, and the personal friendships and habits of thought have carried over into their post-independence army life. Beyond this, however, the military man's professional concerns and his limited budget lead him to urge his country to procure military equipment from the former colonial power whenever possible so as to avoid the added logistic head-aches of mixed weapons systems. The senior officer is likely to feel most comfortable with junior men who received approximately the same professional training as he himself did. This, too, requires staying at least on speaking terms with one's former masters, and limits the opportunities for extensive military relationships with the Communist powers. In North Africa, the difficult conditions since independence and the more extensive Cold War competition have led to a wider set of military relations with outside powers. The larger size of the armies, too, has made it easier to integrate supplies from different sources. South of the Sahara, the military's record seems consistently conservative, although it has not always been decisive. In both Tanzania and Kenya, it is the politicians, not the military, who have sent officer candidates for training in Eastern Europe and who have sought military hardware there. In each case, the military has been reluctant to accept the men and matériel into its organization, and has backed those politicians who have protested. When a country like Ghana has decided to diversify its army's procurement and training ties with outside powers, it has done so by forging new links, primarily with the "white" Commonwealth and India, i.e., with armies modeled on the British pattern.

There is no guarantee, however, that this professionally conservative bias will be effective if the regime decides to act contrary to military advice. Nor should one expect that new generations of officers will necessarily think the same as their present superiors. The most one can say, in summary, is that today such limited influence as the military establishment exerts over foreign affairs is primarily of a restraining and conservative nature.

SECURITY CONSIDERATIONS

Quite apart from any pressures put on the regime by the military establishment, real or imagined threats of national security will affect an African nation's foreign policy. For African nations, even more than for most small nations, it can be stated that their foreign policy, and not the military, is the main instrument of national defense. It is to the organs of international order and cooperation, the United Nations and the Organization of African Unity, that the African states look to guarantee their borders and to which they would turn to repulse serious invasion. Beyond such purely diplomatic recourse, however, many African states have explicit or implicit defense pacts with major powers. France's former colonies have maintained the closest links. All except Guinea, Mali, Cameroon, and Upper Volta have formal defense agreements with the former metropole, and the latter two could probably count on French military assistance if the government requested it. Although French Information Minister Alain Peyrefitte was doubtless stretching the point when he announced, in February, 1964, that French troops had intervened ten times since 1960 to help independent African governments, no one disputes the importance of these agreements for the government in power. The former British colonies have found it less politically advantageous to retain formal defense ties with Great Britain, although, as she did in the case of the East African mutinies of 1963, Britain probably would respond to a call for help from one of her former colonies. Only Liberia, reflecting the continued interest and influence of the United States, has a formal defense treaty with one of the two superpowers. It was occasioned, at least in part, by the Communist military aid to neighboring Guinea. In addition, of course, the United States has unofficially provided direct military intervention in support of the Congo (Leopoldville) central government.

Several mutual security arrangements are or have been in force among African states. The members of the OCAM, the Entente, the former territories of French Equatorial Africa, the Union of African States, the former members of the East African Common Services Organization (EACSO), the UAM, and the Casablanca Group have all at one time or another pledged one another mutual military assistance, though none of these groups, except possibly the Entente, has taken any serious steps toward establishing any visible means of military coordination. OCAM is too new to have done, as yet, any serious military planning; the Equatorial states are too small and troubled; the Ghana-Guinea-Mali Union never really existed; EACSO has disbanded its military high command; and the high commands that the UAM and Casablanca set up never did anything. If the Entente states have arrived at some degree of coordinated planning, it is because they were all within the same French overseas Defense Zone until May, 1965, and the French army command took it upon itself to unify its forces and their local auxiliaries. The Charter of the Organization of African Unity says nothing about mutual security, although it does state that members "shall coordinate and harmonise their general policies" with respect to, *inter alia*, "cooperation for defense and security." It also provides for a Defense Commission, but nowhere commits or urges a member to respond to attack on another member.

The weakness of the military branches of these organizations reflects primarily their over-all organizational weakness, the low priority that military coordination is given, and the great complexity of the job. A few factors have made the military men themselves hesitant about such arrangements. Lack of confidence in security procedures has increased officers' reluctance to divulge data about their forces to allied officers, and the great variation in rates of promotion in the different national armies has complicated personal relations between officers of the various nations. In one case, a major refused to take orders from a colonel in the army of a neighboring state who had been an NCO under the major's command in the old French colonial army.

Militarily ineffective as these agreements may be, they do serve a political purpose. This is a time-honored way of publicly expressing international solidarity, of reassuring one's own people, and of putting would-be aggressors on notice that they will have to face whatever coordinated sanctions and pressures the organization in question can mount.

On at least two occasions, neighboring states have effectively coordinated their military efforts for limited local purposes. Algeria used its army to restrict Tuareg movements across the southern part of its territory so that Mali's army could bring the dissidence under control. Ethiopia and Kenya have mounted coordinated attacks against the Somali Shifta raiders, also with some success. In each case, the common military problem has drawn the states in question into closer diplomatic and political relations, and the success of the operations has opened the door to wider military cooperation. It seems likely that it is in this range of common local problems that mutual security arrangements among African states will have most effect.

Foreign Dependence

Although the military establishment may be the symbol and guarantor of national independence, by its very existence, an African army increases its government's dependence on the outside world. Arms, even the sort that African armies use, are expensive and must be procured abroad. Officers, and often noncommissioned specialists and technicians, must be trained abroad, for the most part. The more modern and effective the army or the branch of service, the greater its dependence on the outside world. Except in North Africa, navies and air forces invariably depend on foreign officers or technicians, as well as on foreign equipment. Were an African army to seek the capability for long-range expeditionary operations, it would have to increase this dependence still further. Even so resolutely independent a country as Mali must go hat in hand once a year to persuade some country to fly its paratroops so that the mass drop can be the *pièce de résistance* of the Army Day parade. Quite irrespective of the personal preferences of the military men themselves, an African government cannot avoid depending on the outside world if it wants a respectable army. If it wants a good army, it must actively increase its foreign dependence.

Such dependence need not hobble a nation's foreign policy completely, nor need it bind a nation to a single patron. Diversification of suppliers is a standard method of spreading liability so that a nation can still offend a great power without fear that its army will be left without ammunition for its rifles. Such diversification must of course be done with care and forethought if chaos is not to result. Aside from logistics and standardization problems, it makes no sense to send men for pilot training to Britain and then give them MIG's to fly. Usually, whole weapons systems and the training to use them must be obtained from the same or a closely related supplier, if they are to be used effectively.

Whether or not a nation seeks to diversify its dependence, its freedom of choice in foreign policy can be constricted. One can at least question which is easier—to stay on good terms with a single jealous patron, or to find policies that will keep a wide spectrum of suppliers with directly conflicting interests minimally content and acquiescent. The fact that most African armies are incapable of mounting a foreign adventure and are used primarily for maintaining domestic order has so far meant that the great powers have not felt it necessary to attach too many strings to the use of their gifts. At the same time, the granting or withholding of favors in the military domain is one more way in which an outside power can hope to exert influence. At least part of the reason why so little of the promised African military aid to the Congolese rebels ever materialized may be that Western powers let it be known that their military assistance programs to the African nations in question might be adversely affected.

Perhaps the greatest form of dependence on major powers is that developed by the former French colonies which had substantial numbers of French troops stationed on their soil. In this case, the dependence was as much financial as military, since the foreign bases employed large numbers of local people, and their expenditure supported much of the local economy. In an extreme case, Senegal calculated that it derived $40 million a year from the presence of French troops at Dakar and Thiès. The reduction, between 1963 and 1965, of French troops in Africa from 40,000 to 6,600 has been a dominant factor in relations between France and her former colonies, and most of the African chiefs of state concerned have followed Léopold Senghor of Senegal in viewing the withdrawal of troops as a symbol of a general loss of interest by France in Africa. If this is so, we may expect to see an increase in independent action in foreign affairs by the French-speaking African states.

It is, of course, possible for a client nation to use its military dependence to manipulate donor nations. Such Cold War blackmail, while always possible, may carry with it very high costs if the first donor nation does not choose to play the game and the alternate donor demands a high price, in political or other terms, for cooperating. Although it is impossible to state it categorically, the Western nations, at least, seem to be increasingly sensitive to this sort of manipulation in the military realm to the point where its effectiveness may diminish decidedly.

The Military as an Instrument of Foreign Policy

Any country will try to use its armed forces to further its foreign-policy goals. A respectable military establishment serves to bolster or increase a nation's prestige in the world arena; somewhat more actively, a country may offer various forms of military assistance to those less well endowed as a means of influencing or rewarding their actions, and when all else fails, a country can use its army to try to bludgeon recalcitrant foreigners into submission. On a small scale, African nations are employing or considering all of these approaches.

The military now seems generally accepted as a symbol of national prowess and strength in Africa. The honor guard, the march-past—or even fly-past—are part of the standard treatment for the visiting dignitary, and some African military units can be quite impressive in their ceremonial functions. Increasingly, generals or at least military aides-de-camp to the president are included in visiting delegations. While it may be taken by all as ritualistic show, it reveals an increasing acceptance of the military's place in the modern nations that African countries wish to become. At a somewhat less superficial level, African nations are quite aware of the size and composition of their neighbors' forces, and the possibility of numerous small-scale but expensive arms races between politically competitive countries cannot be ruled out. France, particularly, and Britain have tried to give comparable military equipment to comparable countries, but their control over total force composition will steadily diminish. West Africa has seen one quiet, but very real, competition in size of forces between Ghana and Nigeria. Although the two countries are of widely disproportionate size, their military establishments have increased at approximately the same rate since independence, with Ghana generally showing the lead. While there is not much immediate danger of the two armies' confronting one another, it is of some political importance for each country that it not get left behind in the competition.

The 1960 Congo crisis provided the first occasion for African armies to play a major role in an international arena, and most acquitted themselves very well. Membership in the Organization of African Unity increases the likelihood that African states will be asked to provide troops for multilateral international peace-keeping missions, and the ability to do so is clearly an important aspect of an African nation's general international prestige. Whether this sort of prestige can be directly translated into concrete diplomatic gains is more problematic. As Ghana found out in the Congo, even having troops on the spot in an international force is no guarantee that one can exercise control over events, or even specify in detail the purposes for which one's own troops will be used. Rather, it is likely that the ability to provide military forces will become the entry price that an ambitious African nation must pay if it is to hope to influence decisions where an international force is involved. This does not in any way decrease the importance of maintaining such troops.

Bilateral military assistance may potentially have greater political payoff, though this, too, is far from certain. The Nigerian battalion sent to Tanzania, at Julius Nyerere's request, to maintain order following the 1964 mutiny was not expected to advance any immediate Nigerian political aims in the East African country, though very likely Nigeria thought to benefit indirectly from the gratitude of the Tanzanian Government, from increased international prestige, and from keeping Ghanaian forces out. The very act of providing military assistance may commit the donor to public approbation of the policies of the recipient and thus restrict the donor's freedom in policy formation. For such reasons probably, the six "moderate" African nations that the Tshombe Government approached for military aid, in August, 1964, found graceful ways to decline, much as in other circumstances the great powers have sought to avoid the stigma that comes with giving public aid to countries with objectionable regimes.

Military assistance may be provided in other ways than by directly sending troops. One of the classic ways is to provide officer training, and Egypt has already offered such training to several African countries. So far, among tropical African countries, only Ethiopia, and only on a very small scale, has been able to offer such training, but President Kwame Nkrumah of Ghana indicated great interest in building up a major military staff college in his country to service all of Black Africa. The political advantages of such a scheme are obvious. Aside from whatever direct influence one could exert over the individual officers who presumably would rise to top command, it would be also advantageous to have military procedures of other African nations standardized to one's own. If one thought in terms of developing a united African military force for defense or liberation purposes, the command would be all the more likely to fall to the nation that had provided the command training. Ghana's continued interest in close military cooperation in Africa was also directly related to Nkrumah's interest in wider forms of political unity.

Officer training at a senior level is very expensive, however, if not in monetary terms then in the human resources and skills that must be diverted to it. Any such senior African officer staff train-ing program would have to be staffed almost entirely by expatri-ates if it were to be more than pure window dressing. Very few African officers, even now, have the necessary staff training, and taking those few to be schoolteachers would seriously impede the day-to-day functioning of their own armies. The use of expatri-ates, however, would seem to undermine the major purpose of the school, and unless the instruction were of a sufficiently high pro-fessional calibre the school would be unlikely to attract the attend-ance and attention that alone could justify politically the outlay of resources. Junior officer training would seem a more promising way for African countries to expand their military assistance, but the very reasons that make it possible to offer such training also make it possible for the individual countries to train their own lieutenants. There would seem to be no particular reason why African nations should cooperate any more in the field of military training than they do in regular academic training, and without such international cooperation it will be difficult for a single nation to derive overwhelming advantage from offering extensive officer training to its neighbors.

The easiest form of military assistance to give is assistance to guerrilla or other irregular forces which are part of a rebel move-ment. Algeria, particularly, and Ghana, to a lesser extent, have given training and arms to groups of freedom fighters from south-ern Africa, and Guinea has helped rebels from neighboring Portu-guese Guinea. States bordering on troubled areas—e.g., Zambia, Tanzania, Senegal, and the Congo (Leopoldville)—have provided shelter and sanctuary but have not been in a position to offer more direct military aid. Aid to rebel guerrillas is likely to be relatively inexpensive since their conditions of operation preclude use of heavy equipment, and also because some wealthy outside donor can probably be found to pay the arms bill in the first place. Such military aid is also heavily political in nature, both in the sense that its most crucial component is political organizational skill and in the sense that the payoff, if the rebellion succeeds, is likely to be very great indeed in terms of the foreign-policy goals of the donor nation. Indeed, much of the planning and execution of assistance to rebels is taken over by political agencies, rather than the military, within the donor nations. That is probably least true in Algeria, where the aid to the Portuguese African rebels has been most decidedly of a military nature and where the army's political role is of long standing.

The need for the high political component in such guerrilla assistance programs became painfully evident in the case of the Congolese rebellion, which collapsed, not for want of arms, but from general political ineptness, lack of organization, and factional bickering at all levels of the rebel organization. The political collapse of the Congolese rebellion and the lack of military success in the Angolan and Mozambique revolts point out that the international prestige and political influence of the donor nation will not necessarily be helped by too close an identification with unsuccessful causes, however politically meritorious. Even success or the hope thereof may have its penalties. Ghana's championing of various rebel causes made her suspect, perhaps a bit unfairly, in several African capitals where frightened and indignant incumbents were inclined to blame Nkrumah for any rebelliousness among their own people. Distrust of the Ghanaian leader unquestionably hurt his country's aspirations to African leadership.

Playing host to exile liberation armies may decisively limit one's freedom of action in both foreign and domestic policies. Tunisia's Habib Bourguiba had to walk a very narrow line when 25,000 soldiers of the Algerian National Liberation Army were quartered on his soil. The presence of the Mozambique liberation group FRELIMO in Tanzania has likewise given Nyerere little option but to follow strongly anti-Portuguese and anti-NATO policies, at the same time that it has raised the fear of Portuguese retaliatory bombing of Dar es Salaam if FRELIMO becomes too active in Mozambique. The exiles' presence has stimulated a heavy inflow of arms into Tanzania, and probably the buildup of the Tanzanian army as a potential counterweight to the rebels in case things got out of hand. Zambia faces a similar problem with armed refugees from Rhodesia, and the Congo (Leopoldville), perhaps feeling that it has enough problems, has withdrawn the sanctuary offered the Angolan National Liberation Army.[5]

[5] I am grateful to John Marcum for bringing to my attention the points in this paragraph.

Sudan, likewise, has become edgy about the use of its territory for distributing arms to the Congolese rebels; and the mysterious arms shipment that Kenya intercepted in May, 1965, produced a major diplomatic incident involving that country and Uganda. The continued support of armed liberation movements seems certain to add an unstable element to the politics of numerous states bordering on troubled areas. It may be partly for this reason that most direct military aid for rebel movements in Central and Southern Africa has come from North Africa, which is geographically insulated from the disturbances.

Ultimately, a nation may use military force to influence the behavior of foreign nations, or even to destroy them and to restructure the international environment. To summarize the present African situation, it is necessary only to say that the opportunities for such direct action to be effective are so limited that the threat of their use is barely credible. As pointed out above, African nations are protected from external aggression by international organizations and by external powers with a stake in maintaining the *status quo* and the ability to intervene rapidly. This protection is reinforced by the military limitations on any African attack force, which to overcome external political and military intervention must be able to produce the effect of a *fait accompli* before outside forces can intervene. Since African forces are weak, the success of external military measures must depend primarily on political revolt fomented from within. Such coordination between internal dissidence and external troop movements is very difficult to bring off and above all to keep secret. The troop movements and similar external pressures may also have the effect of reinforcing people's loyalties to the regime in power, as appears to have happened when Ghana tried to bring military pressure on the Republic of Togo.

The major exception to such a generalization is the case of states under white or non-African rule where, on the one hand, much of the indigenous population might be expected to greet the invading army, at least initially, with open arms, and where, on the other hand, it is possible that no international body or major power would intervene to retain the *status quo*. India's invasion of Goa would be an example of action that could conceivably be repeated for small territories like Portuguese Guinea, Río Muni, Ifni, and the Spanish Sahara. Invasion of the larger white-held territories of Southern Africa would be quite another matter. No single African nation is capable of bringing sufficient military force to bear on any of the major white redoubts to carry the day, and it is also highly unlikely that an international African force could do so. In the foreseeable future, the most that the African nations, including those in North Africa, could be expected to provide is 40,000 troops for such action, even assuming that the colossal problems of coordination, transportation, and supply could be solved. Against these, Portugal could put 60,000 seasoned troops in either Angola or Mozambique without increasing her present effort or leaving one territory undefended. Rhodesia could field 30,000 troops with good air support, although with less training, and could probably count on substantial help from South Africa. The Republic of South Africa has the most modern army on the continent and could quickly field an organized force of 120,000 men which it could soon double without placing itself on a full war footing. It has been calculated that a successful direct invasion of South Africa would require at least 90,000 highly trained men with the most modern armaments, 700 aircraft, and 100 ships and transports. The cost of each month of operations would be about $95 million, and casualties on the attacking side would run from 19,000 to 38,000 killed and wounded.[6]

If some international force were to mount such an attack, the African states could provide only negligible contributions, and there is no guarantee that their say in the final political settlement would be any greater than their military contributions warranted. Only if indigenous rebels were seriously to disrupt the existing regimes of Southern Africa to the point that the will and ability of the whites to defend their positions were destroyed could African forces by themselves hope to make a success of an invasion, even assuming that no outside force chose to intervene.

Much of this paper has emphasized the difficulties and limitations on use of African military establishments. One should not, however, hastily conclude that general military considerations

---

[6] These calculations are presented in Amelia C. Leiss (ed.), *Apartheid and United Nations Collective Measures* (New York: Carnegie Endowment for International Peace, 1965), pp. 150, 165–70.

have and will have no serious effects on foreign-policy decisions. At the very least, these decisions will be directly affected by the military weakness of African states and by their inability to bring military force to bear on problems of foreign policy. Unfortunately, states are more likely to perceive and seek to remedy existing weaknesses than they are to understand the limitations on the action even of increased military forces. If only for this reason, the resources that African nations devote to their military establishments are likely to continue to increase. It is apparent also that military considerations can affect foreign policy only in a highly political context. Military agreements with European powers are part and parcel of other, and more important, forms of dependence. Similarly, to be effective, the use of military force against foreign nations must be dependent on favorable indigenous political conditions, and the most effective way in which an African nation can give foreign military aid is in support of an armed, domestic, political uprising. The African military is thus unlikely to remain completely divorced from politics, even where it is so now.

As noted earlier, most political influence that armies possess is used to secure a suitably large part of the annual budget for their forces. If forces continue to expand, their political influence may grow, or perhaps more seriously, their officers will lose patience because it does not grow fast enough. The simple military *coup d'état* will not necessarily have direct effects on a nation's foreign policy, however, and the variety of conceivable coups makes it virtually impossible to predict what any such effects might be for the continent as a whole. A major effect of the continued growth of armies may be that politicians will feel obliged to devise new ways for keeping their soldiers busy and out of political trouble. The use of the army as a training device for youth and civic action groups, or as an internal engineering and construction force, is popular with political leaders and with some military men in underdeveloped countries. Inevitably, however, such activity involves the military directly with the civilian population (and perhaps with some of its least-satisfied portions) and gives it control over new resources that could be politically activated against the incumbent regime.

To prevent the military from assuming too many sensitive domestic functions, the political leaders may feel it useful to keep their military men occupied elsewhere. It has been suggested that Ethiopia's willingness to volunteer men for international forces may be related to Haile Selassie's uncertainty about the loyalty of his army. Such concern may in the future give more impetus toward direct military involvement with various African rebel movements or toward the formation of some international African force than is now the case. Such an international army would of itself become a major, and as yet unpredictable, force in African foreign relations. Based on current attitudes, some states would almost certainly oppose such military activities unless they were of the most innocuous sort, and the primary effect might be the crippling of such all-African organs of mutual cooperation as now exist.

Quite different and much less discouraging projections could be made. It is not preordained that military forces must grow inexorably, although recent history in most of the world does point in that direction. Even if they do grow in size and political power, as in Latin America, their growth may be accompanied by greater rather than less international stability, although the domestic price may be high. Africa is unusual in that it comes onto the world stage at a period in which it is assumed that new states will not overtly use military force against their neighbors. Such an assumption puts exceptionally heavy burdens on civilian makers of policy. It is largely civilian competence and success that will determine how greatly military factors will influence African foreign relations.

V

Cultural and Psychological Factors

ROBERT A. LYSTAD

The relationship between African "social values" and foreign policy is often acknowledged but seldom explicitly explored or concretely described. There are sound reasons for this. Social or cultural values are not directly observable; they are inferred from people's behavior and institutions. They are useful in explanation or prediction because of the apparent logical congruence between them and the behavior with which they are thought to be related. Despite widespread awareness of their reality and presumed effects, however, culture and values are causally related to alliances or policy differences between states somewhat as ghosts and ancestors are to female fertility and councils of elders: They are perceived as "real"; they are "known" to "influence" action. But precisely how they do so is difficult to demonstrate satisfactorily, and attempts to relate them usually arouse skepticism or dispute about the facts or the relationships, apathy about their researchability, or charges of circular reasoning.

There are other reasons for the difficulty. Social values can be studied most productively on social groups that are comparatively homogeneous and comparatively stable, and that have demonstrated their capacity to survive as systems for at least the full lifespan of a generation. Since the largest social group pre-eminently engaged in the conduct of foreign policy is the population of the nation-state, Egypt, Ethiopia, and Liberia are the only independent African nations that meet the time requirements. When a nation's population is culturally heterogeneous to a degree not character-istic of older and more homogeneous—though socially stratified—cultures, when a society is emerging rather than fully emerged and fairly well integrated, when political and social systems have not yet proved themselves durable and able to adapt to rapid transformation, the possibility of meaningfully relating cultural determinants to foreign policy is greatly reduced. Even in the case of the more homogeneous, more integrated, and more durable older societies, the possibility appears to be only relatively greater, but the difference in degree is important.

Concrete foreign-policy decisions, of course, are made, not by a society at large, but by certain designated smaller groups within it—usually by elitist political and governmental individuals and groups, and perhaps by a few others. Generality and ambiguity in hypothesizing about relations between social values and foreign policy could probably be better avoided if attention were focused on the values of such select groups. If this were done, values of the emergent society-at-large could be generally disregarded, except in specific situations in which the values of a particular local group determined or forced the elite to make a locally necessary deci-sion. The concentration on foreign-policy elites would seem to be peculiarly appropriate for African nations. National foreign pol-icy-making is largely a function of groups that appear to be peculiarly distinct from and unrepresentative of most other social groups; little, if any, positive participation in decision-making is required or expected of the latter. The elite groups often consti-tute a tiny minority that differs from the majority in education, occupation, wealth, successful upward social mobility, experience with urbanism and other aspects of the modern world, and other crucial characteristics. One may presume that the values of this minority also differ markedly from those of most other members of the emergent society and, in fact, they may well be the only significant values.

Although it may be theoretically desirable to concentrate on the values of modernizing elite groups, one who attempts to do so faces certain obstacles. There is the practical problem of gaining access to the elites in order to observe them while they are engaged in the decision-making process. Thus far, elites have been analyzed primarily as they function within their own emerging, fluid social systems; they have not been rigorously studied as actors in an international political environment. It is difficult, furthermore, to estimate the degree or direction of their cultural and psychological biases. Are modernizing elites really very different from others in the society? The question cannot easily be answered when so many groups in these emergent and as yet ill-defined societies are inarticulate or ill-informed or apathetic about international politics or when other groups, for other reasons, are constrained from expressing contrary viewpoints which could reveal their particular underlying values.

Modernizing elites, moreover, are not undifferentiated. French-speaking and English-speaking elites are often distinguished from each other on impressionistic bases. Conservatives, moderates, and radicals; ideologists and pragmatists; activists, gradualists, and legalists; Monrovians and Casablancans; East, West, Central, and North Africans; old and new; first, second, and third generation; and many other subgroups have been distinguished within the broad category of elites. Ambivalences or conflicts in cultural values among members of all the elite subgroups probably produce simultaneous or alternating feelings of love and hate toward the West, for example, or toward members of other elite subgroups. Such ambivalences may engender apparently contradictory policies which reflect apparently contradictory values, some of which may be expressed in one international situation, some in another.

Foreign policies and domestic policies, furthermore, both may be responses to the same external or internal stimuli, and either type of policy may be used to stimulate the other or to rationalize or justify the other. Whether the policies are responses to real needs or are manipulated in a contrived manner to achieve the ends of a particular interest group or individual, foreign and domestic policies clearly influence each other. It is sometimes difficult to tell whether a foreign-policy statement is intended primarily to advise or warn foreigners of impending action or primarily to accommodate domestic groups and maintain their support.

Finally, most outside observers may be incapable of perceiving the logic, consistency, and wholeness of actions and values that are possibly present in African foreign policy. Certainly, few gifted and rigorous analysts and interpreters have clearly related cultural and psychological determinants and social values to foreign policy. This threshold of knowledge of African affairs—and of most other regional affairs as well—remains to be crossed.

CONCEPTS

A number of concepts need clarification before further use is made of them.

Culture

Goodenough has well defined culture as an integrated cluster of standards for deciding what is, standards for deciding what can be, standards for deciding how one feels about it, standards for deciding what to do about it, and standards for deciding how to go about doing it.[1] By learning these standards, the members of a society achieve a common understanding of the world in which they live. The way they organize their experience of the world gives it structure and form. The world they perceive and conceptualize is not necessarily identical with that perceived and conceptualized by an omniscient scientist, but it is the world to which they must relate themselves.

Members of a society also have beliefs about cause-and-effect relationships between the phenomena they perceive in their world. These make it possible for them to explain events and relationships and to devise means of adjusting to them and manipulating them to suit their own purposes. The means of adjustment and manipulation need not be created afresh in every generation. They come largely from the previous generation, which, through precept and example, teaches the more youthful learners what the world is like and how its events can be predicted and its processes directed.

The concept of culture covers a wide range of religious, esthetic, recreational, "refined," or prestigious behavior and other

[1] Ward H. Goodenough, *Cooperation in Change* (New York: Russell Sage Foundation, 1963), pp. 258–59.

activities. In fact, the concept of "political culture" has come to be used to describe what political activities are, what they can be, and how people feel about them. It includes far more than the rituals or symbols of authority, rank, and deference, and accords with the usage of the concept in this paper.

Values, social values, and cultural values

These concepts are used interchangeably to refer to the ways in which members of a society rank events or states of affairs in their world as more or less desirable. Values are those states of affairs for which there is great preference, great intensity of sentiment or emotion, and near unanimity of understanding. The desire to achieve them, which is acquired through the culture-learning process, and the knowledge of the most desirable ways of achieving them, enable an individual or a group to select the best possible modes of action from among all the alternative modes the world seems to present. In a homogeneous, stable society, the values are well understood, widely shared, and by and large, though not inevitably, consistent with each other; together they form what can be called a system of values. They give the members of a society a sense of purpose and the principles for selecting new purposes, consistent with the old, when the always changing world presents new situations and alternatives.

Values do not necessarily impose either severe restrictions on behavior or narrow limits to the permissible variation between groups and between individuals; they serve rather as guidelines or directives for action. In his classic statement, Clyde Kluckhohn wrote:

> There is a philosophy behind the way of life of each individual and of every relatively homogeneous group at any given point in their histories. This gives, with varying degrees of explicitness or implicitness, some sense of coherence or unity both in cognitive and affective dimensions. Each personality gives to this philosophy an idiosyncratic coloring and creative individuals will markedly reshape it. However, the basic outlines of the fundamental values, existential propositions, and basic abstractions have only exceptionally been created out of the stuff of unique biological heredity and peculiar life experience. The underlying principles arise out of, or are limited

by, the givens of biological human nature and the universalities of social interaction. The specific formulation is ordinarily a cultural product. In the immediate sense, it is from the life-ways which constitute the designs for living of their community or tribe or region or socio-economic class or nation or civilization that most individuals derive their mental-feeling outlook.[2]

Although Florence Kluckhohn and Strodtbeck find nothing particularly wrong with that statement, they do criticize it on the grounds that it and certain other concepts it describes ("unconscious systems of meanings," "culture themes," "core culture," "basic personality type," "national character," and others) have stressed only the dominant values of a culture.[3] The variant values that are to be found among different social classes and ethnic or regional groups have generally been overlooked. The concepts, furthermore, have been applied only to single cultures and do not permit systematic comparisons between cultures. Such comparisons are especially necessary for the serious study of emergent African national societies.

Kluckhohn and Strodtbeck studied in a particular, fairly homogeneous, stable society the common human problems for which all peoples at all times must find solutions. Those they regard as crucial are the conceptualizations of human nature, of man's relations to nature and supernature, of time, of activity, and of man's relationship to other men. They have discovered that each subgroup in the society differs from some or all of the others in its rank order of preference or certain value alternatives.[4]

[2] Clyde Kluckhohn, "Values and Value Orientations in the Theory of Action," in Talcott Parsons *et al.*, *Toward a General Theory of Action* (Cambridge, Mass.: Harvard University Press, 1951), pp. 409–10.

[3] Florence R. Kluckhohn and Fred L. Strodtbeck, *Variations in Value Orientations* (Evanston, Ill.: Row, Peterson, 1961), pp. 2 ff. Their study, like most studies of values, unfortunately has only limited and principally theoretical relevance to the study of African values and African foreign policies. The groups they analyze and compare are subgroups within what is essentially a single, small-scale, non-African society.

[4] Expressed in this form, my own values include: (1) a perception of human nature as mixed good and evil but capable of increased good; (2) a perception of nature and supernature as subject to control by man; (3) a perception of time as a continuum in which in some respects the past may relatively be ignored, and in which the present may be enjoyed for itself but should be more largely devoted to the creation of a better future; (4)

This writer is not aware of any comparable research on African traditional societies. Nothing comparable has been conducted on any emergent African national society, or on any other national society, or on the value determinants or on the modernizing elite determiners of any foreign policy, African or non-African. However promising the prospects of such research, furthermore, conclusions are not likely to be reached for any African nation or foreign-policy process for some time to come. Apart from the difficult procedures such research entails, it is likely that the ordering of preferences will not be clear cut for some, or even all, of the values in societies that are undergoing rapid change. African "national" societies are clearly in this category.

Although difficult, it is worth trying an intuitive, impressionistic approach in studying the relationships between cultural and psychological factors and African foreign policies. The foregoing discussion of culture and values has referred to several different but related aspects of the phenomena: the *cognitive* aspect (the perception and conceptualization of structure and order in the world), the *affective* aspect (the positive sentiments or feelings associated with desirable states of affairs), and the *evaluative* aspect (the choices between alternative actions; the selection of purposes; the recognition of what ought to be as well as of what is; what to do, and how to do it).

Individual members of a society or of groups within it are not forced to act: they are not determined or bound by their culture. They are rather culturally inclined to act in certain ways, more likely to make certain choices than others. But because they are only predisposed to do so, they can change their values, they may bring former values into question and into conflict with newer values—sometimes, it appears, "overnight." Within any single society, the values of some groups may be at variance, and even fundamentally conflict, with those of others; from time to time, the values of a single group may even radically conflict with each

---

a perception of activity in which the immediate gratification of impulses and the contemplative control of impulses should be subordinated to the energetic creation of new and better things and relationships; and (5) a perception of man's proper relation to other men as one in which the personal worth and dignity of each individual is so great that he should be left completely free to conform to all the others.

other. And when, as in Africa, the national society itself is ill-defined, only emergent, and striving to operate at a low level of integration, the cultural, psychological, or value factors are uncertain or unclear. Some of the implications of that condition are discussed below and provide much of the substance of the other chapters in this book.

Cultural factors: race- and region-oriented theories

Several concepts have gained some currency in the various attempts to locate the invisible values that influence visible national foreign policies. Among these is the concept of a racial psychology or of a racially oriented regional personality. In its most simple forms, racial theorizers assert that there is a causal relationship between distinctive, genetically inherited characteristics and presumably distinctive qualities of "mind" or personality—in this case an "African mind" or an "African personality." The latter are usually ranked by such theorizers as intellectually and morally inferior or somehow less desirable, if the theorizer is racially different from his subjects; superior and more desirable, if he is racially "identical" with his subjects.

Simplistic theories of this kind are seldom discussed or published by scientists. In one sense, they are hardly worth mentioning. But they are rather widely and popularly entertained outside the scientific and intellectual communities, and they may even receive limited currency within intellectual communities as a learned part of the Western cultural heritage which predisposes even some intellectuals to accept them. If so, the influence of such simple theories is likely to be reflected privately rather than openly, in the superior "knowing wink" of the shared secret understanding, in paternalistic or patronizing attitudes and actions, rather than in the bald assertion of what is known to be a discredited viewpoint. Whether or not the simple racial theories are seriously entertained by many Europeans, Americans, or acculturated Africans, many of the latter doubtless believe them to be influential in non-African thinking about Africans. African foreign-policy makers may even give some weight to this belief-factor in their decision-making; however, one can only *surmise* that they do or feel that they would be justified if they did.

Simplistic theorizing about racial heredity—and its implied denial of any possibility of effecting widespread changes in values or in the direction of quality of action—has been severely criticized by social scientists and is no longer part of the consensus of their thinking about the determinants of human behavior. Man's genetic structure does not include values that predispose action in foreign policy or in any other relationships.

It must be acknowledged, however, that the possible genetic determinants of social behavior are little known. Some probable genetic determinants of some forms of abnormal behavior have been determined, but little can yet be stated about genetic causes of "normal" behavior in any society. Racial theorizers who maintain that there is a rather rigid causal relationship between the genetic and social variables have been criticized largely on the basis of such indirect evidence as the range of variation in action displayed by individuals and groups of apparently similar genetic structure; the overlapping of modes of action between persons of different genetic structure; and the changed characteristics of individuals or groups after they have been subjected to new sociocultural stimuli. Two general areas of knowledge require considerably more buttressing before one can utterly reject what are now totally discredited theories: One is that of the genetic determinants of behavior; the other is that of the precise way in which sociocultural factors intervene to direct or redirect action and values. Until such information is available, one can only agree that the available evidence on correlations between genetic and value variables strongly indicates that the more simplistic racial theories can be ignored.[5] The "African mind," the "African personality," and African foreign policies clearly appear to have no more distinctive a genetic base than does any human quality or activity anywhere in the world.

Not all race-oriented speculations are simplistic in attributing personality and behavioral characteristics to genetic or other biological determinants. The more sophisticated theorizers usually

[5] Representative evidence from psychological research in Africa on these and related problems is reported by Leonard Doob, "Psychology," in Robert A. Lystad (ed.), *The African World: A Survey of Social Research* (New York: Praeger; London: Pall Mall, 1965), pp. 373–415; see especially pp. 375–79.

identify a rather large, undifferentiated group on the basis of its members' biological similarities and on the basis of their living in the same general region. They attribute certain common qualities in terms of similarities in physical environment—climate, vegetation, topography, limited or specialized food and other resources in the subsistence economy, nutrition and disease, or other factors. Similarities of history and similarities of cultural patterns and social institutions—communalism, authoritarianism in political and family organization, statelessness, subsistence economics, witchcraft and sorcery, and others—may also be called on to explain apparent similarities in other characteristics. Behavior associated with these variables, of course, provides the raw data for all studies of social values, but racially oriented or regionally oriented theorizers tend to confuse these nonbiological, environmental, and social variables with the biological variables on the basis of which the group is identified. This only obscures the nature of their relevance.

LeVine estimates that "the cultural variation among the millions of people and hundreds of linguistic groups in sub-Saharan Africa is so great as to defy an attempt to describe 'African culture.' Ignorance of this variation has vitiated the attempts of many nonanthropologists to contribute to culture and personality studies."[6] Above the scale of the tribal region, and in many instances even below that scale—even where urban centers have not intruded into the countryside—the degree of homogeneity is insufficient to permit facile generalizations about the qualities of the African personality. Attempts to attribute a nondescribable culture—and hence a nondescribable system of values—to a genetically, environmentally, and socially heterogeneous African population can only be nonproductive, regardless of the number of nonbiological factors introduced to lend balance and credibility to regionally and racially oriented theorizing.

An esthetically and emotionally appealing effort to achieve the nonachievable nevertheless has been made by those who have cre-

[6] Robert A. LeVine, "Africa," in Francis L. K. Hsu (ed.), *Psychological Anthropology: Approaches to Culture and Personality* (Chicago: Dorsey, 1961), pp. 48–92. LeVine's essay and Doob, *op. cit.*, provide the most competent, comprehensive reviews of psychocultural-social research presently available.

ated the concept of *négritude*—a concept invested with an element of racial-regional theorizing. The creators of the concept suggest that, in addition to the common traditional cultural heritage of a communal life, ripe with joy and spontaneity, in the lush virgin tropical forest where man and nature are one, there is a distinctive quality of Negroeness—a kind of universal system of values—somehow inherent in African and other Negroes. This core of being has been sullied but not destroyed by the colonial conquest and enforced subordination to the "white man's" materialistic, less humane values, and it now strives for free expression in the new African culture.

That this concept need not be dismissed out of hand is indicated in the evaluation by Simon Biesheuvel:

> Négritude . . . is in keeping with the concept of vitality which I consider to be characteristic of the behavior of African peoples. A culture in which this concept concerning the meaning of life reigns, can dispense with an excess of activity . . . such activity is required mainly for sustained effort in pursuit of some self-imposed duty or goal. It has no need of the inner-directed personality structure which Africans are not now likely to develop to any extent, and it repudiates the drive element in work motivation, which is relatively lacking in Africans, as destructive of the main purpose of life. Though essentially a West African creed and in keeping with limitations imposed on human effort by the tropical climate, it is by no means inappropriate to certain features of African personality development at all cultural levels as we have found it here in the South. Indubitably, the philosophy of *négritude* is far more likely to provide the black masses, in their transition from traditionalism, with a meaningful new culture than is provided by the more alien model of the West.[7]

One can conceive of this concept, phrased in this fashion, as providing a logical and psychological justification for a South African political policy of separate development, a use doubtless abhorrent to its original proponents. But that two quite different and insightful persons, Senegalese President Léopold Senghor and Simon Biesheuvel, a South African psychologist, reflecting on the Afri-

[7] Simon Biesheuvel, *Race, Culture and Personality: The Hoernle Memorial Lecture, 1959* (Johannesburg: Institute of Race Relations, 1959), pp. 36–37. Quoted in LeVine, *op. cit.*, pp. 72–73.

can condition from quite different perspectives, should find common ground in the concept of *négritude* suggests that there may be some basis for it in the invisible reality of African values.

Divested of its poetic, romantic language and its emotional and mystical evocations, *négritude's* real references or precise values are difficult to ascertain. LeVine has compiled a list of cultural characteristics that may be said to be "distinctively African, although they are neither limited to Africa nor universal throughout it." They include pastoralism, large and dense populations, highly developed prestige economy and acquisitive culture patterns, centralized political institutions and institutionalized leadership, unilineal descent groups, bridewealth, polygyny and the mother-child household, initiation rites and genital operations, ancestor cults, witchcraft and sorcery, and importance of proverbs in folklore.[8] Are these the actions and institutions directed by the *négritude* inherent in Africans? Whatever may be the answer to that question, *négritude* clearly is not a simplistic racial theory; it is neither racist nor race-hating, despite the ambiguities of poetic vocabularies. But what is it? What core trait or value moves the Africans as it moves no other men?

Without accepting the view that the concept of *négritude* can be validated, Doob hypothesizes that traditional Africans tend to seek immediate rather than future rewards to a greater degree than do acculturated Africans or Europeans.[9] That kind of statement has the virtue of being testable and of suggesting further hypotheses —even about foreign policies—but it hardly stirs the emotions with a sense of tragedy, grandeur, dignity, and hope. English-speaking African intellectuals, in fact, have long displayed apathy toward the concept.[10] Outsiders, not deeply involved in such intellectual issues, may view the concept as an interesting cultural phenomenon and may enjoy or resent the symbols its users employ, but they need not regard it as a cultural factor influencing any kind of behavior. If *négritude* refers to anything identifiable, it probably refers to the conceptualization of the world by certain African

8 LeVine, *op. cit.*, p. 52.

9 Leonard Doob, *Becoming More Civilized: A Psychological Exploration* (New Haven: Yale University Press, 1960), pp. 84–93.

10 Colin Legum, *Pan-Africanism: A Short Political Guide* (rev. ed.; New York: Praeger; London: Pall Mall, 1965), pp. 95–97.

and non-African Negroes as having unjustly become a "white man's world," to the accompanying feelings of frustration and hostility at the injustice and humiliation of having to live in such a world, and to the longing to change such a world by synthesizing the most rewarding of its cultural features and developments with those of an earlier world as it is presumed to have been. That these beliefs, feelings, and evaluations are widespread—though not universal—in Africa is caused, not by biological factors but by the gross similarities of conditions, of history, and of colonial social institutions and values. The two kinds of variables should not be confused.

The absence of any verifiable causal relationship between racial factors and values and foreign policy or other forms of behavior does not prevent Africans—or others—from believing that they are causally related. Culture and cultural values do not require scientific verification for their sustenance. Thus, prolonged and rising frustration in what is perceived as a "white man's world"—whether directly or indirectly experienced—could conceivably cause a high value to be placed on Negroeness or Africanness per se. These simplistic racist concepts—including hostility to all whites, non-Negroes, or non-Africans—may well have already become values to some Africans in some places in some situations, but this writer discerns no universal or even widespread patterns of perception that could be called strongly racist. To a small extent, conceptions of, and attitudes toward, other races and cultural groups have been measured,[11] but the results reveal little about the prevalence of racial stereotyping by Africans. They certainly do not suggest any incipient, simplistic anti-white racism or any particular identification of Africans with darker-skinned or other biologically "distinctive" non-Europeans. The existence of such an identification is not validated by research and is based solely on impressions—which are notoriously poor as data and are readily countered by contrary impressions. But one source of impressionistic evidence—African foreign policies—seems worthy of serious consideration.

No African state rejects "whites." Many highly prestigious roles may be closed to them—but not all. This may be only a temporary

[11] Doob, "Psychology," *loc. cit.*, pp. 405–9.

policy of expediency, but it nonetheless remains a fact. It indicates that African foreign-policy elites continue to use relevant non-racial criteria and that while they reject whites in some situations they accept them in others. More significantly, the foreign policies of African nations toward racially similar African nations are marked, in some circumstances, by similar patterns of allegiance and acceptance, by indifference or tolerance in others, and by acrimonious and bitter rejection in still others.

Such evidence cannot be expected to allay the suspicions of those who believe that, increasingly, Africans are adopting racist values, but at least it can alert more suspicious persons to the oper-ation of nonracial variables in the Africans' valuing process. Al-though the racial factor cannot be totally ignored, one can safely assume that what may appear as racism is better explained by the situational variables of time, place, and sociocultural factors. Isaacs may have aroused controversy with his article on the uncomfort-able status of American Negroes in Africa,[12] but he certainly did not invent all his evidence or present an utterly groundless assess-ment of the attitudes of many Africans toward racially similar but culturally dissimilar groups. His article and the counterassertions to it make plain the need to probe inside or behind the conceptions of whiteness or Negroeness to discover those nonracially oriented values that influence the perceiver more significantly.

National character

Much of the criticism and skepticism generated by racial-re-gional theorizing may be aroused by assumptions about the rela-tionship between national character and foreign policy. Despite the "psychologizing" that frequently accompanies the analysis of political institutions and processes, and despite the often brilliant insights into psychological, cultural, and value aspects of African politics within individual countries—insights one intuitively feels must have some validity—the study of national character has hardly begun.[13]

[12] Harold R. Isaacs, "A Reporter at Large: Back to Africa," *The New Yorker*, May 13, 1961, pp. 105–43.

[13] See Harvey Glickman, "Political Science," in Robert A. Lystad (ed.), *op. cit.*, pp. 131–65.

Alex Inkeles' valuable, comprehensive survey of the literature on national character adopts this widely accepted definition of the concept: "[It] refers to relatively enduring personality characteristics and patterns that are modal among the adult members of a society."[14] Thus far, studies of changing patterns of personality organization among Africans who have undergone various degrees of acculturation have had only limited relevance to the understanding of national characters, which by definition require measurement of national populations. Few African nations have endured long enough to develop "relatively enduring personality characteristics," and their populations are still too heterogeneous to permit generalizations about a national society. To my knowledge, no personality studies have been made of that most relevant group, the foreign-policy elite, and one must be suspicious of generalizations about it that are based on analyses of other acculturated groups. Samples of an acculturated population would not necessarily be representative of what is probably a highly specialized group of foreign-policy makers. In view of the policy differences between African nations, furthermore, a study of one national elite could not be generally applicable to another national elite. Whatever generalizations could be made would require a high level of abstraction. Although Doob's study is one of the most thorough and cautious attempts to reach conclusions about the direction of personality change as Africans become more modern,[15] inferences about foreign-policy makers and their policies based on his hypotheses would require testing in specific countries and specific situations. For a long time to come, such testing will hardly be feasible.

Little more can be said in this context. Because of its greater popularity outside of social-science or other intellectual circles, the frequent confounding of racial and personality variables, and the potential impact of racial hostility or conflict on foreign policies in various parts of the world, racial theorizing has received more attention here than the concept of national character.

[14] Alex Inkeles, "National Character and Modern Political Systems," in Francis L. K. Hsu (ed.), *op. cit.*, pp. 172–208.
[15] Doob, *Becoming More Civilized*.

CULTURAL AND PSYCHOLOGICAL FACTORS IN AFRICAN FOREIGN POLICIES

This chapter will now strike out more positively and reflect, in an admittedly general and intuitive way, on some possible cultural and psychological factors that underlie African foreign policies. With reference to American character and foreign policy, and with specific allusions and statements about relationships, a similar step was taken in 1950 by Almond, in a book reissued with a new introduction in 1960. Among the developments of that decade to which he draws attention are "the climate of *hostility* in which the United States has to operate" and the "cultural qualities of the American business elite which impede its capacity to respond to the challenges of the international situation."

Of the former, he states:

The negative emotions and hysterias unleashed by the disruptive changes and the new nationalisms of the non-Western world seem to require a target, and the United States as the most powerful Western nation must bear the burden of memories of colonialism, as well as the burden of leadership, without permitting these violent moods and expressions of hate to deflect it from a steady and vigorous course.[16]

Of the latter development, he avers:

[The American business elite distrusts] governmental expenditures, except for purposes closely and clearly related to security interests. . . . The idea of a program of foreign aid for purposes of economic modernization in the developing areas . . . runs into conflict with the *quid pro quo* investment culture . . . [The] American business elite lacks an anthropological or sociological sense. Essentially, it tends to believe in the moral superiority of the American business culture over all other cultures. It has tended to think of its own achievement of a high level of material culture through a free-enterprise system as the natural object of emulation for the peoples of the "backward areas." . . . The idea of growth in the non-Western world—economic, social, and political growth—as the central objective of American foreign policy cannot be fully grasped by an elite

[16] Gabriel Almond, *The American People and Foreign Policy* (2d ed.; New York: Praeger, 1960), p. xxviii.

group which cannot think anthropologically and sociologically.
. . . If we are to affect the course of cultural change in the non-
Western areas, we must be prepared to change ourselves, to act out
of "cultural character," to overcome our parochialism and ethno-
centrism.[17]

The observation of the "climate of hostility" relates to a dominant affective or emotional aspect of African and other transitional
cultures. The observation of the need to "act out of character"
relates to a need that must come to be felt in all societies, whether
transitional or established, African or other, and by all foreign-
policy makers. Both concepts, "hostility" and "acting out of character," are, in a sense, the themes of the remaining sections of this
chapter.

One can say little about values that are universally held on an
African continent in transition. It is possible, however, to specu-
late about some of the psychological processes and elements that
are undoubtedly associated with certain values in the personalities
and subcultures of foreign-policy elites and to an increasing extent
in those of the non-elites. Let us then examine what appears to be
one of the dominant psychocultural directives of African foreign
policies. It is found in the affective or emotional aspect of values
(how people "feel" about the world); it is a particular quality of
feeling "hostility" or "aggressiveness" which often appears to be
dominant in the policy-makers and their policies. The cognitive
and evaluative aspects (the *what is*, the *what can be*, the *what to
do*, and the *how to go about it*), furthermore, are discussed more
fully in other chapters of this book.

A dominant affective quality: hostility or aggressiveness

Hostility and aggressiveness have commonly accepted meanings.
They refer to feelings that vary in intensity, in the time and place
defined as appropriate to their expression, and in the forms of behavior through which their expression is socially acceptable.[18] The
feelings are not peculiar or confined to African elites, nations, or

[17] *Ibid.*, pp. xxix–xxx.
[18] See, for example, E. E. Davis, *Attitudes Change: A Review and Bibli-
ography of Selected Research* (Reports and Papers in the Social Sciences,
No. 19, 1964) (Paris: UNESCO, 1965).

foreign policies. They are present in greater or lesser degree, and are at least latent, in every social group and in the foreign policy of every nation. But the internal and external environments in which African nations and elites must live seem particularly conducive to the arousal and expression of these feelings in relatively greater intensity.

Hostility and aggressiveness do not necessarily imply the use of violent force or overt physical or vocal aggression against sharply defined enemies, although these modes of behavior certainly are used in circumstances of extreme frustration. Violence and conflict have been threatened and employed. But it is the reality and nature of the emotion more than its concrete expression to which attention is being directed in this chapter. Hostility and aggressiveness can be expressed in a variety of ways far short of overt conflict, depending upon situations of the kind discussed in other chapters of this book. Moreover, although African countries generally lack certain capacities and opportunities for sustained expression or conflict, they are not restrained solely for such reasons.

Some of the various forms of reaction that can arise from feelings of hostility are illustrated by Kluckhohn and Leighton in their analysis of Navaho Indian reactions to a disturbing, frustrating relationship with white American culture. They include trying to be as like whites as possible; following vocal leaders within Navaho society; participating in factional quarrels or family fights, or in humor and "joking relationships" with certain relatives; phantasizing about witchcraft or attacking witches; engaging in verbal and other indirect hostilities toward whites; suffering fits of depression; physically withdrawing; using narcotics, alcohol, and sex as means of escape; participating intensely in native religious rites and turning to new religious cults; and rigidly compartmentalizing their lives and feelings.[19]

The absence, or only sporadic presence, of violent conflict and aggression in Africa, then, does not contradict the assumption that feelings of hostility are present. Nor is this a case of "damned if you do, and damned if you don't." Unions and agreements between African nations, friendly accords, unanimous resolutions,

[19] Clyde Kluckhohn and Dorothea Leighton, *The Navaho* (Cambridge, Mass.: Harvard University Press, 1946), pp. 113–44.

warm handclasps and smiles before photographers, honorific titles and decorations, and the proffering and receiving of aid do not necessarily indicate the absence of hostile feelings. One can even argue to the contrary that those symbols of friendship and unity reveal the presence of hostility. In the absence of proof, however, one may safely guess that such actions, whether ceremonial or substantial, express mixed emotions which can vary in intensity according to the circumstances.

Hostility and aggressiveness, it should be repeated, are latent, if not always manifest, in the foreign policies of all nations. They are inherent in any social situation in which separate, sharply differentiated groups (in foreign affairs, they are sovereign nations) must compete with one another for scarce values, resources, and means. All such groups experience the blocking or frustration of their desires; they are incapable of achieving perfect integration with one another; they cannot achieve the perfect socialization of their own members; and they are even less capable of creating a sense of identification with outside groups. It is in the very nature of most groups not to try to achieve the latter too completely.

Without sentimentality or moralizing, it can be said that hostility is bred in the situations through which transitional African nations have passed, are passing, and will continue to pass. Doob states the variables in a hypothesis about transitional peoples of lesser social status than foreign-policy elites, but its wider applicability is evident. "In comparison with those who remain unchanged or who have changed, peoples changing from old to new ways are likely to feel more aggressive."[20] The hypothesis is difficult to test and is, of course, subject to qualifying or corollary hypotheses,[21] but it is highly suggestive of the mood of African foreign-policy elites. That mood cannot be ignored, disdained, or extinguished by retaliatory hostility; it is not even extinguishable by "selfless" acts of cooperation. But its intensity is reducible, and the actions to which it gives rise can be made less threatening and more constructive.

Nations are likely to regard submissiveness in other nations as less troublesome and threatening than aggressiveness—apathy or dis-

[20] Doob, *Becoming More Civilized*, p. 80.
[21] *Ibid.*, p. 83.

integration being probably more dangerous because of the vacuum they create. The experiences undergone by African foreign-policy elites, however, have tended to produce active and aggressive rather than passive and submissive policies—a "healthy," if uncomfortable, rather than a deplorable state of affairs. What are some of the experiences of elites in transitional African societies that predispose them toward aggressiveness rather than passiveness, toward feelings of hostility rather than of identity and dedicated allegiance?

Members of the foreign-policy elites are relatively highly acculturated, especially if judged by the standards of the societies that comprise their nations—and this itself is a potential source of hostility. The ordinary citizen (still with more of a legal than a fully achieved social status) may be unaware, or only dimly aware, of the foreign-policy roles, but he nonetheless accords members of the elites high prestige by virtue of their education, relative wealth, possession of the material symbols of their status, association with prestigious foreigners, and ability to perform in national and international ceremonies. In all this, the citizen probably identifies himself with the elites. He also accords them high prestige by virtue of their right and ability to articulate the feelings of hostility that are present within himself in a more inarticulate, diffuse form. Within their own elite group—or at least within their own clique within the elite group—members are also accorded high prestige. This prestige is not necessarily dependent upon their skill in foreign-policy roles; it may be based upon other roles they play, on the allegiance they can command as persons operating in a social system in which many different roles may be played by the same person. The personal prestige of a member of an elite group—as long as it lasts—carries over from role to role, and one means of perpetuating it is to act out the hostility he and the others feel. An attack on an appropriate target relieves his own tension and gives similar relief to his tense associates and to the citizens, who are thereby drawn more closely to him.

Among ordinary citizens or non-elites, the status group often referred to as "youth"—characterized by rapid but not yet equally fully achieved acculturation or elite status—is far more articulate, far more specific in its definition of appropriate targets of its hostility, and far more overtly aggressive than most other status groups. The cultural and psychological sources of its aggressiveness, however, are not different in kind from those of the elites, who, along with most non-African foreigners, are frequently the objects of the youths' hostility.

The process of acculturation that went on for centuries among some African groups has rapidly accelerated since the end of the colonial period. The recent spurt is a product in part of new forces, in part of the "snowball effect" of accumulating acculturation during the entire colonial period. Its effects may be seen in the widespread, though by no means universal, assimilation into African cultures of many items of material culture, etiquette, and manners, and of certain social institutions and standards.

The most important effects, from the standpoint of foreign-policy analysis, however, are the acceptance by the African elites of the concepts of modern science and technology and of the nation-state as the most effective institution for organizing and administering large numbers of people. Tentatively or partially accepted along with those concepts have been the more "basic values" (as some anthropologists would define them): (1) *mastery over nature* rather than subjugation to it or harmony with it; (2) the enjoyment of life as dependent upon the *achievement* of "higher standards of living" *in the future* rather than upon the preservation of past traditions or the pragmatic adaptation to present conditions; and (3) *action* to radically change the human situation rather than indulgence in the immediate satisfaction of impulses or control of impulses and desires through philosophical detachment from ordinary affairs. Science and technology and the nation-state are perceived as the principal instruments by means of which those new basic values can be achieved. The most thoroughly acculturated Africans are theoretically not distinguishable in these respects from the most thoroughly "modern Westerners." But members of this small group are a small minority among the African elites, who are ambivalent about these values.

Culture was defined earlier in this chapter as a concept that includes standards for deciding not only *what is* but also *what can be*. Members of stable societies perceive the latter as compatible with the former, as extensions of the former, and they share knowledge and feelings about what to do to achieve the latter. In transitional societies, the gap between the two perceptions is far greater. An acculturated perception of what can be, furthermore, is not necessarily accompanied by thorough knowledge of what to do to narrow the gap between the real and ideal or of how to successfully achieve a satisfying personal adjustment while having to live with the dissatisfying realities.

It is commonplace to point out that such conditions produce feelings of frustration, anxiety, discontent, or tension. Outsiders who do not suffer the same frustrations, or who suffer them only in small degree, do not usually appreciate the results of such frustrations. For the feelings do not simply remain self-contained until drained off by rational action and its consequent success. These internal "states of mind" engender feelings of hostility and aggressiveness, and through their expression tension is initially relieved and its level lowered. If the personalities of leaders or if domestic policies sometimes appear to be unduly erratic, disordered, or authoritarian, or if foreign policies and policy pronouncements seem unnecessarily hostile, they are attributable, not to the "superficially acculturated" Africans' inherent incapacity to act rationally or in a gentlemanly fashion, but to their profoundly human capacity to react emotionally to their deprivations and frustrations.

One source of aggressive sentiments, then, is the experience of acculturation. Some elements of Western cultures have proved desirable but not immediately or completely assimilable. A second source of those sentiments is in the nature of the culture contact that was mediated largely through the institutions of colonialism. Regardless of the best intentions of colonial administrations and of missionaries, businessmen, teachers, doctors, and others who were an integral part of the acculturation process, the nature of their relationships with the subject peoples precluded complete identification with the people whom they ruled, converted, employed or traded with, taught, or treated. During the same span of colonialism, it was impossible to establish the kind of mutual allegiances to a single unified social group which is capable of obscuring individual differences, controlling aggressiveness, and maintaining consensus and solidarity. Here and there, individual colonialists were capable of achieving a high degree of identification with Africans, and some groups of colonialists were more successful than others. Some small groups of highly acculturated Africans became nearly indistinguishable from their colonialist peers and came to feel more at ease with modern culture than did most colonialists or ordinary citizens of the metropoles. But the problems of achieving widespread social solidarity were too great to be solved during the colonial period.

In normally functioning, well-integrated groups, feelings of aggressiveness are so repressed that an individual is likely to be unaware of them or to deny their existence. The feelings of allegiance that accompany identity of membership, goals, and means are sufficiently strong to overcome feelings of resentment. Members of a group, furthermore, share cultural standards with reference to appropriate expressions of aggressiveness and the control of disruptive behavior. But when, in the absence of a high degree of identity, two groups are forced to interact continually, and when one of them is in a position of power or authority over the other, feelings of frustration and hostility are aroused, however dormant they may lie for a while or however inarticulately they may be expressed. Furthermore, the feelings are reciprocal, for the group in authority feels hardly less frustrated and aggressive; its one advantage is that by expressing or acting out its aggressiveness according to rules it has itself established, it can reduce its own tensions in some degree. Thus, mutual hostility may spiral, unless a sense of movement toward close identification and common culture is achieved. Then the peoples are predisposed to repress their feelings and to direct them into actions that are mutually defined as appropriate and constructive. The high points of the spirals in Africa were reached before mutual allegiance could be achieved.

The positive action of gaining independence has reduced the degree of tension among African elites by inverting the political authority relationships; but not all relationships have been so neatly or quickly transformed. The aggressively declared African hostility to neocolonialism symbolizes the continued existence of a high degree of frustration. This suggests a third source of those sentiments: the gap between what the elites perceive as the potential culture of the entire nation they lead, and for which they are responsible, and what they perceive to be the level of national culture at the present time. A fourth and related source might be identified in the newly perceived scope and difficulty of the problems that must be solved if national aspirations are to be fulfilled.

The perceptions of the two cultures, the real and the ideal, may come to be interpreted by the elites as so fundamentally irreconcilable that only a thorough political and social revolution can possibly achieve the potential desired culture. Traditionalism and political opposition must go; but they do not disappear so easily. Furthermore, an acculturated perception of what can be is not necessarily accompanied by all the knowledge and skills necessary for successfully conducting a social revolution. There are shortages of skilled manpower; resources are limited; interested outsiders may be deliberately hostile or exploitative; and unforeseen consequences create new frustrations.

Outsiders not afflicted with such perplexing concerns tend to rationalize that the gaps between what is and what can be are bridgeable by hard work, patience, self-sacrifice, rational planning, and some infusion of capital and technical assistance. Their view is by no means totally inaccurate. It is deficient in its overstatement of the effectiveness of unqualified rational action and in its overreliance upon certain virtues of character thought to be necessary for success elsewhere. And it is deficient in its overlooking or underestimating the cultural and psychological factors that operate in ill-defined, poorly integrated, poorly equipped transitional societies.

Frustrations are inherent not only in group living or in positions of subordination to the authority or power of alien individuals and groups. They also have sources in the physical environment. Most important, perhaps are the sources in the total social system, some aspects of which are maladjusted to the others and to the environment as it is newly perceived. That is especially the case in societies in which rapid change is occurring or in which the national society is still an agglomeration of at least partially incompatible subcultures and institutions. These are especially frustrating, because the troublesome elements are so difficult to locate. They cannot easily be attributed to any individual or group or any particular thing, because they are obscured by and interrelated with other features of the culture. It is difficult to perceive exactly against what or against whom the hostility should be directed. Or, if the symptoms of maladjustment can be described (e.g., only minor increases in food production, rising unemployment and discontent among school leavers) and some of the causes diagnosed (traditional patterns of land tenure, lack of urban-industrial job opportunities, etc.), the treatment seems too slow and painful to extinguish anxiety. The necessary political measures, moreover, may be unpopular or contra-ideological.

During the colonial period, the rising tide of hostility could be channeled against the institutions of colonialism and particularly against those eminently visible symbols of colonial authority, the colonial administrators and related groups. It was they who exploited the Africans, reinforced or even created new tribalisms and parochialisms, inhibited economic and social development, and denied political self-determination, the one means of unlocking the door to more rapid self-solution of problems. Some colonialists still are present and some still retain considerable authority. The aggressive feelings that characterize policies of anti-neocolonialism stem in part from these frustrating conditions, the continuing colonial presence and the partial dependence upon the former colonial powers and upon expatriates.

But anti-neocolonialism also represents the substitution of a tried and true target of hostility for targets that are too diffuse or hidden to be perceived easily. While colonialism flowered, it could be attacked directly. Now that it has withered or is withering, it serves as a conveniently visible and vulnerable substitute object of hostility for many frustrations not directly attributable to it.

The present generation of leaders attained their status in part through their successful attack on colonialism, and a procedure so rewarding is not easily abandoned as long as, and even after, some of the vestiges of the period remain. Second-generation leaders and the forthcoming third generation have acquired their fundamental perceptions and conceptualizations of the political environment partially through direct experience of colonialism, partially through indirect experience—that is, through learning from and believing the first generation's and previous hostile generations' interpretations of colonialism. The visibility of that target seems already to be diminishing as some nations perceive advantages in ties with the metropoles and successfully repress their hostility, but the concept "neocolonialism" is far from extinguished.

A noncolonial power like the United States may be perceived as neocolonialist in its intentions and actions, because it and the American people are readily identified with the colonial powers. The contrast between its great power and the small power of African nations also reinforces the image of the United States as a threat to their newly achieved status. The perceived similarities between its status and that of the former colonial powers dominate the image and obscure the differences. Anti-neocolonialism, therefore, should not be disdained as simply the hocus-pocus of desperate politicians trying to rally domestic support in order to remain in power. It is more properly understood as another example of the use of a common human mechanism for gaining relief from tension through the display of aggressiveness toward a substitute class of objects. If its side-effects include maintenance of the allegiance of potentially discontented cliques, so much the better.

These three sources of frustration—personal acculturation problems among elites, the colonial nature of culture contact, and the persistent great gap between the present national culture and what is aspired for it—are not the only ones that could be explored. They do, however, indicate what appears to be one of the dominant affective aspects of some dominant cultural directives of African foreign policy.

Conclusion: The Several Faces of Hostility

There is no doubt some danger of faulty communication when so much reliance is placed upon concepts like frustration, hostility, and aggressiveness. Many persons regard hostility as reprehensible; they believe it is wrong to feel hostility, wrong to act on the basis of the feeling, and unjust to be on the receiving end of it. They feel that groups or individuals who display hostility, and nations that incorporate it into their foreign policies, should be reprimanded or restrained—without violence, of course. As used in this paper, however, the concept refers to nothing reprehensible *per se*.

As a consequence of their being social and hence subjected to restrictions, all human beings feel hostility; it is a universal, basic emotion. One can try to control the mode of expression, but one need not deny the reality or decry the morality of the emotion.

The concept of hostility itself provides no means of distinguishing between Africans or any other groups; by itself, it does not differentiate between Englishmen, Ghanaians, Portuguese, Angolans, Belgians, Congolese, Frenchmen, Senegalese, Guineans, Chinese, and Americans, or between the elites and the non-elites of any nations. The clusters of frustrating situations that produce it, however, do enable one to distinguish between the groups. Whatever the distinctive sources may be in specific situations in Africa or elsewhere, it is the limited purpose of this paper to call attention to the common emotion they arouse and to the directive it provides for action. For all human beings, hostility is a kind of surging energy, unpleasant to experience and difficult to contain; the individual and the group must act in some manner so as to release it and enjoy relief.

But hostility does not automatically lead to conflict. The foreign-policy environments discussed elsewhere in this book indicate various ways in which this flow of energy is channeled into other, less hostile forms of action. The widely used concept of sublimation refers to the psychological process by which hostility is directed into behavior that can lead to greater identification between groups or at least into behavior that is socially more acceptable. The policy of nonalignment, for example, could be analyzed with reference to the concept of hostility by conceptualizing it as a mode of action that simultaneously deflects hostility in two or more directions. The effect is one of achieving partial identification with several groups where greater identification with only one would produce greater hostility toward the others and a higher over-all level of hostility. However frustrating the policies of nonalignment may seem to all groups, that over-all level does seem to be reduced. Thus, the double deflection of hostility certainly can be counted by most groups and individuals as beneficial —although some would assert that it is only an immediate, illusory benefit rather than an ultimate, real one.

The policy of striving for Pan-African unity or for more immediate regional unities can also be perceived as a presumably beneficial structuring of hostility. It can be interpreted as a conscious effort to suppress hostilities within the continent or as a positive effort to achieve such identification between African nations as to make possible the automatic, unconscious repression of hostile feelings. In either case, the policy of Pan-African unity can be regarded as the kind of channeling of hostility in which every mature, healthy individual and group continually engages. The African policy of working through the U.N. is another instance susceptible to this line of analysis.

Finally, it must be pointed out that African nations structure their hostility beneficially through direct, rational attempts to solve the problems themselves, through economic development, educational, and other programs that figure so prominently in the shaping of foreign policies. In no African instance can the frustrations be said to have produced elites or national populations characterized by apathy, extreme states of paranoia, or withdrawal from the attempt to solve the problems of culture change.

Nations with lesser or fewer frustrations (because their problems more largely have been solved) should devise foreign policies that make clear their appreciation of cultural and psychological processes, and should display a sophisticated intention to "act out of character," if necessary, in an effort to change the conditions that produce the frustrations.

VI

Political Determinants

L. GRAY COWAN

For all the newly independent African states, the creation of a foreign-policy position to go with their sovereign status has meant embarking on a voyage in rough and uncharted seas. The new governments were faced with so many pressing internal problems stemming from the political and social upheaval accompanying independence that, initially, foreign-policy making of necessity occupied the attention of the leaders of government to a substantially lesser degree than did questions of domestic policy. With rare exceptions, the new governments lacked trained personnel either for representation abroad or for the foreign office at home. Under the pressures of nationalist politics, no one could take the time to reflect upon future foreign-policy positions. Precise definition of the long-term national interest was lacking; the overwhelming immediate need was to preserve the new state from attack by both external and internal forces. As a result, the foreign policies of the African states have been to a degree characterized by *ad hoc* decision-making which, because of the absence of foundations on which to base an over-all foreign policy, tended at times to be contradictory and often to be confusing to the outside observer. The single-party political structure, combined with the presence of a pre-eminent political leader and the collegial nature of the decision-making process, makes precise delineation of the factors in the making of foreign policy more than usually difficult.

We are concerned here with the problem of intra-African *political* determinants, but such political determinants cannot be neatly separated from determinants deriving from economic or cultural factors. What may appear to be a political determinant in a particular foreign-policy decision may well, in fact, be no more than a manifestation at the level of political decision-making of much more deep-seated economic or cultural factors. Thus, for example, political decisions on foreign-policy questions relating to attitudes toward former colonial powers may be conditioned by largely nonpolitical factors deriving from continuing economic dependence or cultural ties. A particular foreign-policy position may reflect personal convictions or cultural ties of the members of the leadership group which have little or no obvious connection with the problem under consideration.

An attempt will be made in this paper to confine the discussion to those foreign-policy determinants that derive from the political situation within individual African states and those that derive from the political relations of the African states within the African community. The determinants of foreign policy in the new African states are often obscured because the distinction between foreign and domestic policy is difficult to establish. Activities and decisions, which on the surface fall within the realm of foreign policy, may well be designed as much or more for internal consumption as for their effect on relations with other states. Foreign policy may be used as an instrument of internal policy to bolster the image of the national leader at home or as a mechanism to create internal political integration and solidarity. Kwame Nkrumah of Ghana, for example, used the threat of an attack by neighboring Togo to reinforce popular support for the concentration of greater power in the hands of the Convention People's Party. The appearance of the national leader at intra-African or international meetings increases his prestige at home. Moreover, the reaffirmation of sovereignty for domestic purposes has frequently been accomplished by the use of a foreign-policy stance that clearly emphasizes the independence of the African government in the world arena. At times, also, a radical stance in foreign policy may be a substitute for the leader's inability to carry out a radical program in domestic policy.

The interconnection between foreign and domestic policy has not infrequently given rise to misinterpretations of the foreign-policy positions of the African states by the outside world. Extreme foreign-policy statements by African leaders which were designed for internal consumption have brought about accusations of irresponsibility or inconsistency. Specific foreign-policy positions taken by African governments must be evaluated in the light of the domestic pressures being exerted on the leadership at any given point. The commitment of the national leader to a particular domestic image may, in fact, be more of a political determinant of foreign policy than the external situation itself. What may have appeared to many observers as an exaggerated reaction on the part of many African leaders to the American-British-Belgian rescue mission in the Congo can be partly accounted for by a natural response to what was considered an unwarranted interference in African affairs by the former colonial powers. Also, in great part, it must be seen as a public reassertion of independence by the African leaders for the benefit of their fellow-countrymen. The subsequent violent attacks on American policy, particularly in the East African countries, are a further manifestation of the use of a foreign-policy issue to reinforce the popular image at home of governments determined to maintain a position of independence and neutrality.

The Congo rescue mission illustrates a further characteristic of current African foreign policies. In general, foreign-policy decisions are conditioned by previous decisions which form a pattern and which serve to restrict the field for new decisions. But occasionally a particular event, such as the Stanleyville rescue, or the mutinies in East Africa, brings about such strong reactions that it forces abrupt changes in direction of foreign policy.

Foreign-policy making in Africa is in some measure hindered by the absence of an experienced diplomatic corps and the comparatively restricted representation permitted by slim national budgets. But these factors are compensated for by the frequent personal contacts among the leaders. African heads of state are inveterate travelers; formal or private visits to neighboring states take place almost continuously. Views are exchanged between old friends; the result of these *tours d'horizon* is a much greater degree of policy coordination, particularly within the French-speaking groups, than might otherwise be expected. Continent-wide meetings of heads of state take place annually and there is a constant round of conferences of lesser importance among the senior civil servants. Outside information is exchanged within the African bloc at the United Nations.

This emphasis on personal communication tends to add a strongly individualistic note to African foreign policies. Personalities play an important role in diplomacy, and the central role of the leader as the formulator of foreign policy is thereby enhanced.

INTERNAL POLITICS AND FOREIGN POLICY

The independent African states today are, with few exceptions, the products of successful nationalist revolutions. In greater or lesser degree, depending in part on the bitterness engendered by the nationalist struggle, both internal political structures and foreign policies are conditioned by the postcolonial situation. It is perhaps difficult for non-Africans to comprehend fully the fact that for many African leaders, the psychological realization of independence may not yet have been fully achieved, although the objective fact of political independence exists. Frequent allusions to the problem of psychological independence are to be found in the writings of African leaders and in contemporary African literature. Perhaps because of the heritage of the French policy of cultural assimilation, references to the need for complete psychological separation from the former colonial power are to be found more frequently in the speeches of the French-African leaders. Sékou Touré of Guinea, for example, repeatedly returns to the theme of emancipation from the modes of thought engendered by colonial subservience, and lays constant stress on the party as an agency for restructuring mass thinking about Guinea's role as an independent African state.

The drive to assert the newly won political independence, which is the fruit of nationalism, and the need to achieve unchallenged international recognition of sovereignty frequently find themselves blocked or frustrated by the economic realities of the postcolonial period and by the lingering sentimental ties of attachment to Europe of many of the present generation of African leaders. For African policy-makers today, the dilemma of both internal and external policy is that the dependence on outside economic aid for development simply cannot be squared with the goals of the African revolution. To accept outside economic aid, no matter from what source, or however minimal the strings attached, represents, psychologically, a degree of infringement upon independence. The African leaders are, of course, objectively aware that no country can be entirely self-sufficient, but the necessity for aid in almost every aspect of the national economy creates, for the African governments at this particular time in their development, an overly acute sensitivity to dependence on external support.

The problem becomes even more complex when a choice must be made between accepting aid from a former colonial power and aid from sources that are disinterested in principle, if not always in practice. On the one hand, the government of the former mother country is at least a known quantity with whom it is easier to negotiate than with an unknown power; on the other hand, behind this form of economic aid there lurks the ever present (and sometimes perhaps justified) suspicion of neocolonialism. The continuing French dominance in such countries as Gabon and Ivory Coast appears to some African governments as an object lesson in the dangers of neocolonialism. There can be little doubt that at least one of the attractions of Chinese help for the young technocrats of the Congo (Brazzaville) regime was the prospect it offered to reduce dependence on the French treasury. From the eloquent example of the Congo, the leaders are fully aware of the dangers of aid that would involve them in the Cold War. Yet they have little alternative to setting a course between Scylla and Charybdis because, without the prospect of substantial economic aid for development, the problem of maintaining internal political stability becomes little short of insoluble. Popular expectations of the material benefits of independence, created in no small part by the nationalist parties themselves in the years of the anticolonial struggle, demand at least partial fulfillment. The future political security of those now in power requires concrete and public evidence of accomplishment; for this, external economic assistance is a prerequisite. The continuing need for aid forces certain compromises with the ideals of total independence and in some measure narrows the spectrum of choices open in the selection of foreign policies.

An equally powerful force determining the course of foreign policy is the need to preserve the ideals and goals of the African revolution. Those who share most passionately the ideology of revolution have repeatedly proclaimed that it will not be complete until the entire continent is free of colonial control and all African countries have attained majority rule. Fulfillment of the goals of the revolution also requires, in their opinion, a commitment to a form of socialism which, through an equal sharing of the products of economic development, will ultimately replace the exploitation of the colonial system. It is claimed that only with the attainment of the goals of the revolution will the true independence of Africa be realized. This is not the place to argue the validity or the practicality of the goals of the African revolution in the form expounded by their strongest proponents, Nkrumah, Nasser, Touré, and Keita. We are concerned rather with the effects that commitment to revolution have had on the formulation of foreign policies.

The general goals of the African revolution, as they have been enunciated since 1958 by Nkrumah, are shared in large degree by all the new independent regimes. The problem lies not in the objectives but in the degree of commitment to them by the various leaders, and their interpretation of the means by which these goals should be reached and the sacrifices they or their countries should be required to make. To the leaders most deeply committed to the socialist revolution in Africa, the goal is not simply rapid modernization. They feel, with an almost missionary spirit, that the pattern of change which they advocate will bring about a profound social transformation that will ultimately restore dignity and equality to the former colonial subjects. It must encompass the continent; only through total and explicit acceptance of the revolution by all states will the African community finally gain an internationally recognized status and dignity. In Nkrumah's eyes, the revolution cannot be confined to one or to a few countries because it is the instrument of genuine African unity. Its failure in one country, he has repeatedly implied, is to be seen as its failure everywhere. Every African regime should be concerned with its success in every other state and is consequently justified in taking steps to protect it where it has occurred or to foster it where it has not yet been fully realized.

Moreover, if the revolution is seen as a unified whole, its failure in one country constitutes a threat not only to African unity but, even more importantly, to its success in every other country. The desire to foster and extend the revolutionary dynamic to the governments of all the African states is intimately connected with the desire to preserve the image that Nkrumah created of himself as a leader whose goals were those of every African. If it could not be proved that the revolution, as it was taking place in Ghana, could be exported to the other states of Africa, then there was no reason to assume the continuing faith of the masses in Nkrumah's own regime.

The duty imposed on those whose commitment is greatest is to advance the cause of revolution wherever possible. Foreign policy viewed in this light becomes an instrument of revolutionary purpose. Not only must the revolution be fostered by encouraging the masses of the other African states but, where leaders show themselves unsympathetic to the goals of socialist African unity, actions that are designed to dislodge them are entirely justified. The fact that such actions are viewed as subversive by the leaders against whom they are directed is regarded only as conclusive proof that they are seeking to block the legitimate aspirations of their people. Ghana has been accused, as have Egypt and Algeria, of actively supporting groups in neighboring states seeking to overthrow their governments. In recent treason trials in Nigeria, Upper Volta, and the Ivory Coast, Ghanaian connivance with those charged with treason has been strongly asserted, apparently with conclusive proof. At the February, 1965, meeting of the heads of the states belonging to the Organisation Commune Africaine et Malgache (OCAM) in Nouakchott,[1] the Ivory Coast presented what it claimed was "irrefutable" proof of Ghanaian intervention in its internal affairs. In a communiqué of March 8, 1965, the Bureau Politique of the Parti Démocratique de la Côte d'Ivoire repeated the charge and threatened not to permit repre-

[1] *Cf.* fn. 8 *infra.*

sentation of the Ivory Coast at the Accra meeting of the Organization of African Unity (OAU), even though Nkrumah had offered to expel from Ghana all the rebel leaders of Niger, Cameroon, Upper Volta, and the Ivory Coast who had taken refuge there.[2] The Bureau's statement concluded emphatically, "We were not liberated from the tutelage of developed countries just to put ourselves under the authority of a country that is certainly no more developed than we are."

The almost messianic element in their devotion to the socialist revolution by the leaders of Egypt and Ghana has created parallel problems in both the Middle East and sub-Saharan Africa. In both cases, it has brought about a sharpening of the split between the revolutionary and nonrevolutionary states within the orbits of Egyptian and Ghanaian influence. It was one of the major forces stimulating the creation of the former Brazzaville, Casablanca, and Monrovia groups. The nucleus of the Casablanca Group, Ghana, Guinea, and Mali, were those states of West Africa most fully committed to the African revolution. The cooperation of Egypt and of Morocco may have been due to a variety of special and individual interests, but the ideological basis for the existence of the group was the commitment to Pan-African socialist aims. The Monrovia Group, composed of those whose commitment to the revolution was distinctly less intense, owed its existence largely to the necessity felt by the moderates to respond to the dynamism created by the commitment of the Casablanca members. The two groups revealed distinctly different political styles in their internal affairs and different approaches to the question of African unity. While both groups formally went out of existence with the establishment of the OAU, the major differences between them survive under the thin veneer of unity represented by the new Organization, and fundamental divergences in style and conceptions of political organization remain. If the OAU proves ineffective in promoting wider union, these differences

[2] *Afrique nouvelle*, Dakar, March 11, 1965, p. 3. It is interesting to note that in a subsequent letter to the Ivory Coast Government, Nkrumah admitted that no other country would accept these rebels, and he offered to "park" them in the north of Ghana on the occasion of the forthcoming conference.

could well break forth again, shattering the fragile shell of the Addis Charter.

Nasser's commitment to Arab socialism succeeded in splitting the Arab states in a way that lined up the conservative members— Morocco, Tunisia, Jordan, and Saudi Arabia—against the Arab states whose leaders shared his convictions. The split between Syria and Egypt which dissolved the U.A.R. may be partly attributed to the fact that, in general, the Syrian leadership never shared the same degree of revolutionary commitment as did the Egyptian; an analogy (which cannot, however, be pressed too far) might be the drifting apart of Guinea and Ghana which led to the dissolution of the Ghana-Guinea union. The slowly growing *rapprochement* between Guinea and other former members of the French West African Federation, represents a threat, not only to the solidarity of the socialist states, but to Ghana's internal political structure.

A second consequence of the commitment of Nasser and Nkrumah to revolutionary goals has been the parallel isolation of the two countries from their neighbors. Egyptian influence in North Africa has continued to wane in the same manner as the influence of Nkrumah in intra-African politics south of the Sahara. In some measure, this increasing isolation can be attributed to the clash of goals between Nasser and Nkrumah. Both were seeking influence in the world of nonaligned states; both saw possibilities of opening wider markets for the consumer-goods industries rapidly being developed at home: both sought the influence which they hoped would come from revolutionary brotherhood —in the case of Egypt, the brotherhood of Islam and Arab socialism; in the case of Ghana, the brotherhood of African socialism. The efforts of the two leaders to expand their influence in Africa canceled each other out and resulted in the diminution of power of each. Moreover, both the African and the Middle Eastern states began to suspect an element of national irredentism in the revolutionary dynamic. Growing concern over the real motivation behind the revolutionary zeal of the two leaders (based upon evidence of subversion) tended to reinforce the disenchantment with the doctrine of political unification.

While the desire to increase the pace of the African revolution was clearly a determinant in the foreign policy of Ghana (as it was for the Arab revolution in Egyptian policy), it was, from time to time, equally useful as an instrument to reinforce the legitimacy of the domestic regime. As Professor Zartman has pointed out, the Moroccan haste to publicize a radical policy by convening the Casablanca meeting is attributable not so much to King Hassan's personal commitment to a revolutionary dynamic of any kind but rather to the need to find a means of meeting the opposition demand for more rapid changes in Moroccan internal policy. The growing personalization of power in both the East and West African countries has meant that the ideological orientation of the party leader and of his immediate circle has become an increasingly important determinant of foreign policy. The leader's personal vision of the type of society he is seeking to create becomes a major factor in the elaboration of domestic policy and in the influence that he seeks to exert on neighboring states through foreign policy. With the virtual disappearance of an opposition and the imposition of governmental control over the mass media, less and less attention need be paid to public opinion on foreign-policy questions.

Although the leaders do not have to contend with mass reaction on questions of foreign policy, the views of the younger group of aspiring politicians surrounding the head of government can be a powerful factor in determining the future emphasis of foreign policy. An illustration of this point is the recent speculation concerning changes in the foreign policy of Tanzania; whether the more aggressive neutralism recently exhibited by the Tanzanian Government represents a change in the personal position of President Julius Nyerere or is the result of pressures exerted on him by influential members of the party is not yet clear, but it is highly doubtful that the government is responding to a massive shift in Tanzanian public opinion toward either the East or the West. In a few instances, domestic pressure groups with international affiliations (such as student groups or the members of the All-African Trade Union Federation) may exert a limited influence on foreign policy, either independently or through the party.

Because of the continued emphasis on the personal role of the leader in the strong executive type of government that exists in so many of the new African states, official attitudes on foreign-policy issues may well reflect the strains and stresses that are present within the political party. Wide domestic dissemination of foreign-policy statements by the leadership is often used to reinforce party directives at the lowest level, especially in Guinea. Conversely, external reactions to particular foreign-policy positions receive little or no coverage in the domestic controlled press if they present the party leadership in an unfavorable light. Foreign-policy issues have also been used to divert public attention from failures at home, particularly in the economic sphere, and to counter internal threats to the security of the government. Nkrumah, for example, used the threat of external attack to consolidate domestic support in the face of severe internal economic crises. Similarly, Félix Houphouet-Boigny used the issue of Ghanaian aggression to help justify the repression of antiparty elements in the Ivory Coast.

Along with the negative use of foreign-policy positions to reinforce internal stability, foreign policy can, of course, be an important positive element in bolstering the political integration and national unity of the new states. The government of Nigeria reaped substantial benefits from the use of Nigerian troops in the United Nations operation in the Congo. Reports of the effectiveness of Nigerian forces in the United Nations operations were given full publicity in the Nigerian press, and public opinion reacted warmly. Subsequent letters to the editor in various papers indicated a genuine expression of national pride. The whole affair was interpreted as a reaffirmation of the importance of Nigeria's role both in the United Nations and in internal African politics. Several correspondents portrayed the use of Nigerian forces as the first real proof of the genuineness of Nigerian independence, and urged that Nigerian foreign policy could be made even more effective were it backed up by a fuller expression of national unity and confidence in the domestic policies of the government.[3]

The direct relationship between domestic and foreign policy in many African states is often difficult to ascertain; but the in-

---

[3] For Nigerian opinion on world affairs, see Lloyd A. Free, *The Attitudes, Hopes and Fears of Nigerians* (Princeton, N.J.: Institute for International Social Research, 1964).

direct relationship of foreign policy to domestic political stability is substantially more important than might be assumed at first glance. The identity of ideological views at both levels is immediately obvious in the revolutionary states, but even the more moderate regimes have not hesitated to invoke foreign policy as a means of reinforcing their domestic position. When Sir Abubakar Tafawa Balewa of Nigeria was accused of subservience to his former mentor, the Sardauna of Sokoto, he seized upon the issue of Northern disapproval of Israeli aid to consolidate his position in the South. By overriding the objections of the North, he demonstrated his independence of Northern influence. The determinants of foreign policy may well be much more closely associated with the immediate internal goals and aspirations of the regime than with a long-range assessment of the national interest in foreign affairs.

FOREIGN POLICY WITHIN THE AFRICAN COMMUNITY

The new states of Africa are now in the process of developing foreign-policy positions vis-à-vis other members of the African community and the non-African world. As vested national interests come somewhat more clearly to the fore, foreign-policy attitudes will probably show an even greater degree of differentiation. Because of their common background of a nationalist struggle against colonialism, however, the new states have hitherto shared two general foreign-policy objectives: African unification and neutralism in their extra-African relations. The latter objective has been closely tied to the problem of security for the state, both internal and external.

At one time or another, almost every African leader has emphasized the necessity of neutrality[4] for his country in the struggle between the ideologies of the Soviet Union and the United States. For many, African socialism represents the neutral ideological path, since it can combine and adapt the best elements from both

---

[4] The distinction between the terms "neutralism" and "nonalignment" becomes somewhat more fuzzy in current African usage. Some states, such as Nigeria, take the official position that they are neither neutral nor nonaligned but "independent" in their foreign-policy stance. For the sake of convenience, I have used the term "neutral" throughout.

ideological systems. African demands for neutrality stem from a variety of factors present in the postcolonial situation. The recently independent states have viewed a position of neutrality as one that demonstrates their freedom from political dependence upon the West. More recently, there has been a growing tendency to see neutralism as a protection from the equally dangerous incursion of influence from the Soviet Union and China. In a speech at Daloa, Houphouet-Boigny expressed his fear of the Chinese in these terms:

> At Nanking in China, they teach Africans how to assassinate those whose eyes are opened to the Chinese peril so as to replace them by servile men who will open the gates of Africa to China. That which colonialism never did—that is, kill the African soul—these men will allow the Chinese to do. It is against this that we are fighting.[5]

While there is common agreement on the advantages of a neutralist position, the same degree of unanimity has not been reached on the methods by which neutrality may be guaranteed. Because of their fear of the possible reassertion of imperial power through economic neocolonialism, the so-called radical states have tended to embrace a more "dynamic" type of neutralism than the more conservative states that belong to the Monrovia Group. This dynamic neutralism, best illustrated again by Ghana and the U.A.R., has frequently taken the public form of exaggerated charges of Western interference in African internal affairs. On the other hand, Communist-bloc interest in the internal politics of African states was regarded as a legitimate expression of concern by those countries which had publicly supported African nationalism from the outset and which, being Marxist, could not, by definition, be imperialist.

The determination of Nkrumah and Nasser to maintain a consistently anti-Western position, at least for external consumption, has frequently led Western observers to express doubts regarding the genuineness of African neutrality. These and other African leaders have been accused of using neutralism as nothing more than a smokescreen for adherence to a pro-Soviet position. There

---

[5] For the English text of the speech, see *Problèmes africaines*, Brussels, No. 272, February 11, 1965.

is much more evidence from both East and West Africa, that a vast majority of African leaders are not only sincere in their adherence to neutrality, but are determined to structure the foreign policy of their states in such a way that their position becomes a matter of public record. Sékou Touré of Guinea openly accepted Marxist principles, thereby exposing himself to the charge of making his country the first Soviet satellite in Africa. It was not until Guinea expelled the Soviet Ambassador in 1961 for interfering in Guinean affairs that the Western powers finally began to accept, at face value, Touré's reiterations of a neutralist stand. More recently, in East Africa, Kenya's neutrality was reaffirmed in the acrimonious debate in the Kenyan Legislature about the illicit importation of weapons from the Chinese People's Republic which might be used ultimately to overthrow the legal Kenyan Government. Farther south, President Nyerere of Tanzania was suspected of having abandoned his previous moderate neutralism when he accepted an invitation to visit the Chinese Republic. However, the public speech he delivered in Peking on his departure was an admirable expression of the neutral position. In it, he pointed out, "We offer the hand of friendship to China as to America, Britain, Russia and others . . . we shall see for ourselves what China's intentions are toward us, we shall not be told by others." A further note of realism crept into his comments on the exclusion of the Chinese Republic from the United Nations, which he termed, "rather a painful reminder that perhaps many of us in Asia, Africa, Latin America and Europe are less independent than we claim to be."[6]

The desire for a neutralist stance has been a determinant of the foreign policy of the African states since their independence, based on a realistic appraisal of their position as weak, new states in the international community. Nkrumah has emphasized that African neutrality is not to be interpreted as a withdrawal from the responsibilities of membership in the international community, but rather as a disinterested position that will enable the governments of Africa to decide upon individual foreign-policy issues with the utmost possible freedom. None of the great powers disagrees with the premises upon which this basic African policy

[6] Quoted by Colin Legum in the *Washington Post*, March 18, 1965.

rests. Whether the African states can succeed in maintaining at least a semblance of neutrality in the face of the pressures exerted on them from the outside is open to speculation. Quite apart from the perfectly legitimate desire of the African leaders to be identified with neither ideological camp, and thereby avoid the risk of destruction in the event of a hot war, a position of neutralism may also be viewed as a temporary but nevertheless fairly long-term substitute for a system of common defense and security.

Every African state is confronted with the dual problem of devising a security system to protect the regime from internal subversion, military uprising, or revolution, and to offer protection from external attack. Given the more or less equal military weakness of all the new states, the prospect that any one would be in a position to mount a successful attack upon its African neighbor is comparatively remote. The real threat of external attack, if there is one, comes from outside the African continent; against such an attack no African state, except the Republic of South Africa, could presently defend itself. This is not to say that sporadic outbreaks of warfare between members of the African community will not take place, chiefly in settlement of specific border claims. As the Moroccan-Algerian border dispute of 1963 and the continuing unsettled conditions along the Somali-Ethiopian-Kenyan border indicate, the African states are no more immune from fraternal strife than are any other members of the international community.

It is highly unlikely that, in the foreseeable future, the OAU will be in a position to maintain a full-scale collective security system. Indeed, the limitations imposed upon the Organization by the underdeveloped military capabilities of most of its members, as well as the restrictions imposed on the powers of its administrative secretary-general by the members themselves, would seem to preclude any effective action on the part of the OAU except in a mediative or arbitrative role in the settlement of intra-African disputes. The primary usefulness of the OAU will not be in the security field but in the development of agencies of intra-African economic, technical, and cultural cooperation. If, in the present divided state of the African community, it tries to do more, the Organization is liable to remain, in the words of Doudou Thiam of Senegal, "a forum of hollow verbalism and outdated phrases."

The African states are dependent for the security of their national existence not on any organization created by themselves but upon European-based and oriented security systems of which the former colonial powers are members. The leaders of independent Africa may resent this enforced relationship, but at the same time it may be preferable to dependence upon a system of collective security under the OAU over which the individual African state might have relatively little control and which would not have the reliability of European power. Although African leaders will continue to stress the necessity of developing an independent intra-African security system, as long as the European powers are prepared to include the African states within European-based systems, no strenuous efforts will be made, particularly by the French-speaking African states, to eliminate the guarantees offered by Europe. The danger is not that African security will be threatened by the continued ability of new states to call upon the forces of the European powers, but rather that the ex-colonial powers will conclude that the cost of retaining the African states within the structure of their security systems will be greater than they are prepared to bear. So long, however, as the financial cost of security can be borne outside Africa, the present security arrangements against external aggression are adequate, if unpalatable, to most African leaders. But the cost of this security in prestige and internal political support may become higher than these leaders can afford to pay. The existence of the bilateral defense pact with France helped to maintain President Léon M'Ba's position in Gabon on one occasion but it is by no means certain that French assistance can be counted on indefinitely.

To some degree, a substitute for reliance upon European-controlled security systems for African defense may be found for the African states in international police actions of the nature undertaken by the United Nations in the Congo. In general, international action aimed at the preservation of either external or internal African security is much the more acceptable alternative, both because African states are thereby enabled to participate in intra-African police measures without the financial burdens involved in mounting the actions themselves, and because international actions avoid the exclusive participation of the West in African affairs. But the advantages gained through United Nations action are substantially reduced by the fact that the U.N. response to a specific dispute cannot be guaranteed. United Nations efforts at settlement are susceptible of being blocked by interests entirely outside the African continent and, even when they are undertaken, they can be slowed down or delayed to the point where they may be of little or no assistance in settling an immediate issue. From the African point of view, a further disadvantage of total reliance on U.N. action is that the ideological split in the United Nations may exacerbate a similar split within the African community. Under these circumstances, African agreement on the proper course of action leading to settlement of a dispute may be difficult, if not impossible, to secure. Thus, while the African states may be in complete agreement on their preference for the organizations to settle disputes—i.e., first, if possible by the OAU, and second, by the United Nations—the only certain sources of immediate security support are still the armed forces of European powers.

More pressing than the problem of external security in Africa today is the protection needed against internal insurrection, whether deriving from purely domestic dissatisfactions or from the encouragement of subversive activities by a neighboring state. Internal insurgency, as a threat to the stability of present African political regimes, may take the form of tribal revolts or military coups, or even the impulsive action of a small, armed group of dissidents. While the possibility of tribal uprisings may be considered somewhat less of a threat to the central government of most states, except in such highly disturbed areas as the Congo, nevertheless, even those states that appear to be most stable, such as Nigeria, can by no means escape the specter of tribal revolt, as the recent upsurge of Yoruba nationalism in Western Nigeria and the disturbances in the Tiv area in the Northern Region clearly indicate.

Experience in recent years has demonstrated that the armed forces represent a further critical threat to internal stability. In most African states, the foundations of legitimacy which the present regimes have built are not yet sufficiently deep to prevent

their being easily undermined. The officer corps of the armed
forces constitutes a technically educated, hierarchic elite, which
has a strong sense of corporate identity and a deep pride in its
accomplishments. It will not stand idly by and watch an incom-
petent civilian government immobilize the process of modernization.[7] The armed forces and the police in all the new African
states represent the only disciplined and organized forces upon
which the governments can rely. The possibility of subversion of
the army leadership, either from the outside or by dissatisfied elements within the country, represents a continuing domestic
danger. The increasing possibility of a military coup aimed at the
overthrow of an existing government faces the African leaders
with a serious problem of foreign-policy decision-making, the
most pointed illustration of which arose in the case of the Tshombe
regime in the Congo.

The more radical African governments made it clear that they
were prepared to extend armed support to the rebels seeking to
overthrow the Tshombe Government. Whatever the personal
feelings of the majority of African leaders may have been toward
Tshombe as a leader, the activities of Algeria, the Sudan, the
U.A.R., and Ghana in support of the rebels in the northern part
of the Congo presented the moderate leaders with the problem of
whether to stand by and see the overthrow of what was, at least
from one point of view, the legitimate regime in Leopoldville.
The answer to this question, given at the founding meeting of the
OCAM early in 1965, was to extend an offer of aid to the legal
government of the Congo.[8] This expression of support did not
necessarily mean that leaders of the group had changed their
minds with regard to the acceptability of Tshombe as the legitimate leader of the Congo, but rather that they recognized the
importance of support by the African community of states for the

[7] The role of army officers in the change of leadership in Dahomey late
in 1965 substantiates this contention.

[8] The new organization emerged from a meeting of fourteen African
heads of state at Nouakchott, February 10–12, 1965. It marked the renais-
sance of regional organization within the framework of the OAU, based
upon the membership of the former UAM. A meeting of the former group
of radicals, held subsequently in Bamako, indicated that the Casablanca
Group might also be reborn under a new name.

legal regime of any member. The principle of respect for legal governments, regardless of the political stance of their leadership, was deemed to be more important in the creation of intra-African solidarity and stability than identity of views on the future course of the African revolution. A recent rash of attempted military coups and the frequent exchanges of accusations of subversion have tended to create a stronger emphasis on the attitude best represented by "There but for the grace of God, go I." Every African leader has become increasingly aware that if the possibility of the overthrow of a regime is commonly accepted, he himself may well be the next victim.

At this level, internal and external policy in the African states are closely connected; the desire on the part of the African "revolutionary" to promote sympathetic regimes in other African states is increasingly counterbalanced by the urgency felt by the more conservative African leaders to preserve the *status quo*, or at the least to ensure that changes in government take place through an institutionalized process of choice and not by violent overthrow. The case was succinctly stated by Houphouet-Boigny in his Daloa speech:

> With the exception of Ghana, Guinea and Mali all the other non-Arab countries on the western side of Africa are either neutral or on the side of the legal Congolese government; while on the eastern only Tanzania, which is rapidly becoming a Chinese "sphere of influence" and to a lesser extent Uganda, openly support the rebels. It can be said therefore that the supposed "dislike" of Tshombe by African Nationalists, of which so much is heard in the Western press and chancelleries, is in fact limited to a noisy minority of at most half a dozen out of the thirty-five independent African states, and that the overwhelming majority are coming to recognize him as just as representative a "Nationalist" as Lumumba, and one moreover who, because he is constructive and not destructive, is likely to do much more for his country.[9]

It does not, of course, follow that the more conservative leaders in Africa have lost interest in the completion of the African revolution through the liberation of those areas of the continent still under colonial control and the forced change of the government

[9] Text cited in *Problèmes africaines*, No. 272, February 11, 1965.

of the Republic of South Africa. One of the major objectives of the Charter of the OAU, to which all the leaders of independent Africa subscribed, was the continuation of efforts to free Mozambique and Angola, and to replace the present white-dominated regime in Rhodesia with majority rule. The instrument established for this purpose was the Liberation Committee, whose task was to coordinate efforts of the African community toward these ends. Funds contributed by members of the OAU to assist the nationalist movements in these three territories and in South Africa were to be distributed by the Committee, and the Committee was to oversee the training of the guerrillas and the care of refugees from these areas. The accomplishments of the Committee have, thus far, fallen considerably short of the expectations expressed at its inception, primarily because of the limited financial contributions that the members of the organization were in a position to make. Also, the work of the Committee has been hindered by the failure of certain members of the parent organization to contribute to its work because they disagreed with the methods and extent of support to be given by the Committee. The more "radical" states favored the "radical" faction of the nationalist movement in such areas as Angola, while others favored support for those nationalists who were less deeply committed to the socialist viewpoint. Here, as at so many other points in intra-African politics, the division between revolutionaries and moderates appeared; the Ghana Government, for example, accused the Committee of failing to support genuinely revolutionary action, and withdrew its active support of the Committee's work. The Committee has recently voted to put its funds at the disposal of the Tanzanian Government since Dar es Salaam is the center of southern exile nationalist organizations.

It has been clear that the present military establishments of the African states are too limited to mount a frontal attack in particular, on South Africa, or on any of the present colonial areas in Southern Africa. While there has been occasional discussion of the possibility of a combined assault by the African states on South Africa, no responsible leader has given official support to an enterprise that, under present circumstances, would be patently foolhardy. In consequence, any material support offered by the African states to the South African nationalist movement will, in large part, take the form of clandestine assistance.

The objective of aid given to internal resistance movements in South Africa would not be in the first instance to overthrow the present South African Government. The internal security system of the regime is so tightly organized, and the powers of the government to oppress antiapartheid agitation so extensive, that there would be little real hope of successfully replacing the Nationalists. Rather, the goal would be to make the cost of maintaining the present apartheid system so high in the face of continued harassment that the regime would be forced to make some concessions to the African majority. Such an expectation might, however, be somewhat more realistic in the case of the Portuguese territories than in the case of South Africa since the power of the South African Government is much greater than the power of Portugal in Africa.

But even this limited form of support for Southern African nationalism from the Black African states to the north presents dangers for the African community. Not all of the independent African states are in a position to be actively identified with Southern African resistance; Malawi, for example, continues to be dependent on access to the sea through Mozambique, and therefore Dr. Hastings Banda's contribution must of necessity be limited, although there is no doubt of his ideological and emotional commitment to the ultimate goal of Southern African independence.[10] Nor can the wholehearted support of Basutoland, Bechuanaland, and Swaziland be counted upon once they have become independent. While there has been some discussion of the possibility of the use of these territories as bases for the organization of guerrilla attacks on South Africa, their economic dependence on the Republic severely limits their usefulness to the nationalist movements. This is particularly true of Basutoland and to a lesser extent of Swaziland. Bechuanaland is more favorably situated as a base of guerrilla operations, but it could scarcely afford to cut off the South African outlets for its meat products without being assured of an alternative export route.

The leaders of independent Africa are aware, also, that their

[10] It may also be argued, of course, that from Banda's point of view, the presence of a stable Portuguese regime that can continue to ensure Malawi's access to port facilities is preferable to an unstable African regime that might not. Hence, the Malawi Government may not necessarily regret the limitations presently imposed on its desire to liberate Portuguese territory.

emotional commitment toward the liberation of Southern Africa may well entail eventual conflict with the cardinal principle of neutralism. Both the Russians and the Chinese would be prepared to support a campaign of agitation in Southern Africa, but their interests in doing so would by no means necessarily correspond with those of the African states.[11] Although the latter might welcome any kind of outside assistance in their campaign against South Africa, the establishment of anti-Western bases in that part of Africa might well have serious consequences for the future of African relations with the West and for the African unity movement as a whole. Also, the possibility cannot be discounted entirely that if South Africa were to feel sufficiently threatened by the combination of forces aligned along its northern border, the Republic's government might feel impelled to take offensive measures against the states organizing those forces. To the West, the probability of such a course may seem slight, but some African leaders have expressed concern about such a possibility.

For the independent African states, the problem of Southern Africa represents a continuing source of irritation. It stimulates an emotional reaction because it represents a blatant public denial of the ideals of African freedom. It exacerbates their relations with the West, particularly with Great Britain and the United States, because the West has failed, in the African view, to join with them to take action necessary to end the dominance by a white minority. It creates a danger to African unity and neutrality because it further accentuates the division between those who would base their foreign policies on immediate and collective action to remedy the situation and those who are restrained by considerations of the possible and the practical. More than any other issue of African internal politics, the emotional appeal of the South African problem excites mass support in Black Africa, and therefore, those leaders who do not wholeheartedly support the more radical demands for collective African action against South Africa find themselves subject to increasingly severe criticism at home, particularly from the younger, educated groups who are able to

---

[11] For a discussion of the goals of Chinese penetration in Africa, see "Le Dossier de la pénétration chinoise en Afrique," *Problèmes africaines*, No. 272, February 11, 1965, Sect. IV.

use this issue as a lever to exert pressure for a stronger "African" foreign policy.

It is difficult to assess, in precise terms, the degree to which African foreign policies today are subject to political determinants since many of these are derived ultimately from nonpolitical origins. The single most important political determinant would appear to be the degree of commitment on the part of individual leaders to African unity and to the African revolution as it is embodied in the ideology of African socialism. The fact that these two objectives, along with neutralism, are the generally accepted determinants of foreign policy may be less important than the varying views of individual leaders on the ways in which the objectives may best be achieved. The difference in African foreign policies is not one of aims but of methods.

The personalized nature of African leadership, combined with the latitude in decision-making afforded the leader who is both the head of state and the head of a highly organized political party, means that any established pattern of foreign-policy decisions may be quickly upset by idiosyncratic action on the part of one individual. As long as foreign policy is used as an instrument to reinforce an internal political image, the factors determining foreign-policy decisions in any country must be seen in terms of the regime's attempt to maintain itself in power at home. Nkrumah placed the blame for Ghana's domestic discontent on the imperialists and neocolonialists who, in Nkrumah's words, "sought persistently to destroy us and the things for which we stand." The neocolonialists were accused of seeking to destroy the nation and the ideology of socialist unity for which Ghana stood. In the view of the revolutionary states, foreign policy is an instrument for protection against those real or imaginary external forces. The need to preserve and further the revolution becomes a determining factor in political decisions in the intra-African arena.

The other major political determinant, the need to preserve the *status quo*, increasingly becomes the key to the foreign policies of the conservative states. The desire to preserve relations with the former European mother countries is closely allied with this, particularly on the part of the French-speaking states, for economic,

security, and cultural reasons.[12] The *status quo* and the domestic
stability of the conservative group can best be preserved by constant watchfulness of the subversive activities of those states that
seek to overthrow legal regimes and to replace them with those
whose commitment to the revolution is more reliable.

Those basic political convictions that determine the attitude of
one group of African states toward another carry over into African relations with the international community. The OAU has
been weakened by the continued divergence of viewpoints on
such issues as the Congo, and the African posture of neutrality has
been endangered by the attempts of the Chinese and the Russians
to establish bridgeheads of influence in the minority of "radical"
states. Correspondingly, the conservative states, which are in the
majority, have only recently become much more suspicious of the
real motives behind the appeal of the revolutionaries and have
sought to isolate them from the main currents of intra-African
politics. The incursion of Chinese influence has helped to open
more widely the existing rift between the two African camps and
has made the conservatives even more determined to resist what
they regard as the threat from the ideological left.

The consequence of the growing isolation of the revolutionaries
has been to make their propaganda more strident and their positions more extreme. But it has also diminished their once popular
support among the younger educated groups in many of the conservative states. The conviction that the only true road to African
unity and socialism lies in the teachings of the revolutionary leaders
has become less marked[13] as a greater number of the younger men
begin to have a personal stake in the existent structure of power.
For the influence of the radical leadership has continued to decline
in almost direct proportion to the number of years since independence, as divergent national interests of the new states become

---

[12] In early 1965, copies of the French satiric newspaper *Le Canard en-
chaîné* were seized in French-speaking Africa because of its critical opinion
of de Gaulle. At the OCAM meeting in February, 1965, it was proposed
that de Gaulle be asked to make a state visit to the capitals of the member
states.

[13] The prestige of Ghana and Guinea, examples of the success of the
revolutionary socialist system, have been damaged by growing evidence of
their severe financial distress, although the present situation is by no means
entirely of their own making.

more firmly established and a greater premium is attached to maintaining the *status quo*.

The commitment to the dynamics of revolution can be expected to determine African foreign policies for some time to come. Whether, in the over-all picture, the influence of this factor will be replaced by considerations of a largely economic nature will depend in part upon the way the revolutionary and conservative groups meet popular expectations with regard to development and distribution of the product growing out of this development. But in the longer run, the attraction of the revolutionary states should not be underestimated. Their efforts to create a distinctive role for the African states in world affairs and their emphasis upon a united African community may prove to have a greater influence on the new generation of African leaders than the cautious and sometimes hesitant approach to the realities of African independence taken by many of the generation of nationalists now in power.

VII

External Political Pressures

C. T. THORNE, JR.

The dissolution of the European colonial empires in Africa, along with the emergence of some three dozen successor states, has been only one aspect of the vast change in the international political system since World War II. At the same time, broader, underlying patterns have determined the conditions under which these states have entered the world and their role in international politics.

THE GENERAL DETERMINANTS

The reshaping of the international political system

First and foremost has been the diminution of Western power in the non-Western world. By the end of World War II, it was becoming clear that, for a complex of reasons, the European colonial empires in Africa and Asia could no longer be maintained. All the reasons may still not be clear to us, since they are embedded in recent history, but one reason clearly was that the European states, temporarily exhausted by the second major conflict in twenty years, simply lacked the will and the power to maintain their empires by force. In sum, time had run out: the great colonial empires of the modern age had proved to be remarkably short-lived.

Two countries emerged from World War II as the strongest

powers in the international political system—the United States and the Soviet Union. They were not merely "great powers" in the conventional sense. They were "superpowers" that had at their disposal enormous strength and were capable of bringing it to bear in every quarter of the world. At the end of World War II, these two powers faced each other: the U.S.S.R. determined to rebuild herself from the wreckage of the war, to take advantage of her territorial gains and of the general exhaustion of the European countries, to press her campaign of world revolution; the United States, somewhat reluctantly and uncertainly assuming the role of a world power, and finding the leadership of the West suddenly thrust upon her.

The U.S.S.R. did not simply emerge from World War II as a superpower; she was also the center of an international political movement which sought to propagate the Communist system throughout the world. The Soviet Union emerged onto the world scene—one might say went from the defensive to the offensive—at a time when Asian and then African nationalism was successfully asserting itself against rule by the West. Thus, two revolutions—independent of each other although not altogether lacking historical connections—challenged the West simultaneously: the revolution of Asian and African nationalism, and the evolving Communist revolution. Subsequently, we shall see that the coexistence of the two revolutions had important consequences for African international relations.

Africa's material dependence on the outside world

Technologically, Africa, taken as a whole, is still the least advanced of the world's major areas. As a result, all African countries must depend substantially on the outside world for the resources and expertise needed to develop the modern sectors of their society and economy. They depend not only on manufactured capital and consumer goods, but also on technical skills, the training of cadres, the provision of modern arms, and the maintenance of currency systems, to mention only a few areas.

Thus, from the very beginning of their independence, most African countries have had to maintain relations with one or more developed states which required an intimacy of a sort not common to "old" state-to-state relationships. The effects of these relationships are manifold; three of them seem particularly noteworthy in this context:

1. *Diversification*. Perhaps the first concern of most independent African regimes is that their dependence on the outside world must be diversified. Prudence, reinforced by internal pressures, dictates this. The most striking result is an "instability" or uncertainty in foreign policies that is perhaps more apparent than real. Some African states seem continually to be maneuvering within the framework of a policy of diversification, alternately making gestures to the East and the West. The aim is to receive benefits from as many outside powers as possible, thus insuring the fewest restraints on freedom of action. The process itself is as old as the history of international relations, but in the case of modern Africa it has particular interest because it involves relationships between extremely weak states on the one hand and the most powerful states of the developed world on the other.

2. *The dichotomies of African foreign policy*. Another result of Africa's material dependence on the outside world is the so-called dichotomy in the foreign policies of many African states. All African states have a natural impulse to assert their sovereignty and independence. Yet, they must respond in some degree to the imperatives of modern Africa—anticolonialism and Pan-African solidarity. At the same time, they have vested interests that often run counter to these imperatives in their overseas relations. As a result, one can sometimes detect different levels in their foreign policies, i.e., levels of declaratory and pragmatic policy. Neither level, or approach, is "insincere," but neither is wholly compatible with the other. For example, Algeria and Ghana, for all their anticolonial activism, somehow manage to retain surprisingly beneficial relations with their former metropoles.

3. *Frustration*. Dependence on the outside world creates frustration and resentment since the dependence exists within a context of vigorous nationalism and unfulfilled aspirations. These frustrations give a meaning both to the rhetoric sometimes employed by African leaders and to actions that are sometimes regarded by the outside world as "irrational."

Africa's political dependence on the outside world

Given their material weakness, the African states cannot achieve some of their collective political goals without the assistance of outside powers. For example, despite the efforts to "Africanize" it, the Congo peace-keeping operation in 1960 depended to a considerable extent on the logistical support of non-African countries. This was not only because non-African states were drawn into the Congo operation for power political reasons, but also because the very existence of a peace-keeping operation depended on resources that were not at the disposal of the African countries, singly or collectively.

The ending of the white regimes in Southern Africa is an objective to which all independent African states are committed, although with varying degrees of zeal. However, the ability of the African states to accomplish this goal by themselves is limited. They can try to isolate South Africa, Portugal, and Rhodesia in the international community. But to do so, they must work through the great powers, because only they have sufficient power to achieve an objective of such magnitude. Thus, in many respects, the African campaign against Southern Africa is a campaign to bring pressure on outside powers—and especially the West—to achieve a result which Africa by itself is still too weak to achieve.

External influence on the African state system

One of the preoccupations of the emerging African state system is to regulate the involvement of outside powers on the African continent. Thus, on the part of the African states, the concern for unity reflects a desire to create sufficient strength to establish the terms under which non-African powers will be involved in Africa. For example, one goal of the Organization of African Unity (OAU) is to create a peace-keeping system which will allow African countries to mediate intra-African disputes and handle peace-keeping problems of the continent. The efforts to create a strong African state system based on an accepted principle of unity are often associated with the "radical" or "activist" states. But in fact, a good many African countries of varying persuasions also support this effort, even though they may disagree with the radicals on the system which should emerge or the powers against which it should be directed.

Leverage through weakness: a paradox

Africa's needs and weaknesses obviously invite the involvement of non-African powers in African affairs. But paradoxically, this creates opportunities for African states to exert leverage on the outside world, a situation that African leaders sometimes exploit with great skill.

Despite its problems and complications, Africa is of considerable importance to the outside world. To a considerable degree, its importance derives from the Cold War. In the past few years, the rigid patterns dictated by the Cold War have been broken by the "thaw" in relations between the Soviet Union and the West, by the Sino-Soviet dispute and the rise of "polycentrism" in the Communist world, and by the emergence of competing power centers in the West. But allowing for all this, the Cold War is still a primary determinant in international politics. For both sides, the underdeveloped areas are of vital importance. First, the attitudes of the "neutrals"—African and Asian—have a considerable bearing on the freedom of maneuver of the great powers. Both East and West must in some degree be responsive—or appear to be responsive—to the opinions and sentiments of the international community, and the neutrals have frequently tried to assert themselves as the conscience of this community.

Second, both the East and the West see Africa as an important area of competition, not for military but for political reasons. For the Communist world, these considerations are more imperative, or at least more clear-cut, since its goals and programs are more concrete. But both the Communist world and the West see Africa as an area where success is measured in terms of how faithfully their societies are reproduced by the developing countries. Perhaps both sides will be disappointed in this hope, but in the long run the West, with its less dogmatic tradition, might better be able to accommodate itself to the disappointment than the Communist countries.

A third reason for Africa's importance to the outside world is that both sides in the Cold War are wary of situations that could escalate into great power confrontations. In the Congo situation in 1960, perhaps some tentative steps were taken in the direction of a great power confrontation. Since then, both the West and the Soviet Union seem to have exhibited caution in that respect. Neither side really wishes that kind of involvement in Africa and therefore in a negative way, Africa is important to the non-African world—as an area where direct confrontations are to be avoided. For Africa, this situation is advantageous; the temptation for the great powers to engage in the most dangerous type of maneuvering, with attendant risk of African countries being "locked in" on the side of East or West, is reduced.

Finally—and this is the factor hardest of all to express clearly—Africa is important to the developed countries of the world in a moral sense. Among the developed countries, there is a sense of obligation to Africa. Like all obligations that find their expression in relations between states, it is obscured, distorted, and frustrated by the exigencies of power. One is struck, nonetheless, by the fact that Africa has caught the sympathy of the developed world. The effects of this on state policies are uneven and complex. But somehow there is an appreciation of the odds against which African leaders struggle, and of their aspirations. Growing out of this is an awareness that the developed world, in its own interests, must foster African hopes in the interests of the whole international community. A result of this awareness has been the setting of certain guidelines, inchoate though they may be, as to how the outside world should involve itself in Africa, therefore influencing the situations and policies to which the African states themselves must respond.

Limitations on the outside world's influence in Africa

Apart from its importance to the outside world, there are certain aspects of present-day Africa that determine the manner and degree of the outside world's involvement in the continent. There are also certain factors that limit the outside world's influence and that act as determinants of the freedom and initiative of African countries in their external relations.

(1) The cruder forms of coercion are becoming less efficacious. There are increasing liabilities to gunboat diplomacy in an age in

which small countries have means of bringing pressure to bear on stronger powers, and in which the grosser forms of intervention can lead to international complications. Perhaps most important of all, both West and East have learned that the only sort of relationships worth having in Africa are voluntary, not coerced. This does not mean that outside powers do not exert pressures. They do, indeed. But the carrot has become as important as the stick and everyone knows this, including the African leaders. France could afford to chastise Guinea without detriment to its over-all position in Africa, but in how many more cases could it afford a similar policy? Belgium counted on an independent Congo's being tied to the former metropole by bonds of extreme dependence. But the formula did not quite work. The price Belgium has to pay for her continued presence in the Congo is to give Leopoldville a voice in how the relationship will be maintained.

(2) The outside world has learned that it is not quite as easy to impose patterns on Africa as was once supposed. When the colonial era came to an end, there was probably a tendency to overestimate Africa's receptivity to outside influence and to believe that, because Africa needed so much, it would model itself according to non-African precepts and patterns. But in fact, Africa tends to resist the imposition of alien influence. Obviously, Africa is and has been subjected to a constant play of outside forces. But the "borrowings" often work out differently than the lenders suppose they will, and tend to become "Africanized." That they do so is not a direct determinant of African foreign policies, but rather a determinant of the context in which policies are made. It is also a "lesson" that is increasingly obvious to outside states seeking to exert influence in Africa.

(3) In political terms, there are obstacles to exerting leverage on African countries. To the outside world, a "presence" in Africa is important as an index of power, prestige, and national interest, and fluctuations in presence are a gauge of how well one is doing vis-à-vis one's competitors. The residual British or French presence in a former African dependency is a guide to how successfully the old intimacy of the colonial tie has carried over into a new relationship. Presence frequently takes the form of what the outsider can do for an African country. But because it is as important to

the former as to the latter, it does not necessarily give the donor leverage in relation to the recipient—not, at least, in proportion to the scale of the presence.

An outside presence often gives an African state a means to exert pressure on the donor. The magnitude of the Belgian presence in the Congo gives Belgium influence there, but it also gives Leopoldville a degree of influence over Brussels. In the first years of Guinea's independence, economic aid from the Soviet bloc gave the Communist countries a special position in Conakry. But those countries also took upon themselves responsibility for sustaining Guinea's economy, and when they faced the usual intractable problems of economic development, they found that presence did not necessarily equal influence. On the contrary, they had in effect given Guinea leverage over themselves, for in order to maintain their presence they were forced to meet Guinean conditions concerning the conduct of aid programs.

(4) Finally, Africa's very fluidity limits outside involvement. Present-day Africa has a tendency both to defy categorization and to change with extraordinary rapidity. As a result, outside powers are wary, uncertain, or hesitant about becoming too closely committed or deeply involved. Although this ought not to be overestimated, it does restrain external influence and thus enhance the maneuverability of the African countries themselves.

How Africa is drawn into non-African problems

The external determinants of African foreign policy cut both ways. Not only do outside influences affect African foreign policies, but they also draw Africa into problems and situations outside of Africa. Although African countries generally tend to resist, they are inescapably drawn into problems that do not directly impinge on the African continent. The Cold War offers familiar examples; for instance, to decide which China or Germany or Viet-Nam to recognize involves a non-African problem. There are also pressures from nearer home. The northern tier of the continent is Arab as well as African, and whether the North African states want to or not, they must in some degree support the common Arab position against Israel—a commitment which can be widened, as the controversy over Bonn's establishment of relations with Israel showed. The participation of African states in "third world" diplomacy similarly exposes them to pressures from outside states seeking to mobilize support against antagonists—for example, Indonesia and Malaysia, Cyprus and Turkey, India and Pakistan.

THE WEST AND AFRICA

The network of relations between Africa and the West

Historically, sub-Saharan Africa's relations with the outside world in modern times have been relations with Western Europe. Despite the common bond of Afro-American culture, the relationship between Africa and the United States was hardly important until the 1950's, when, as the colonial dependencies began to gain independence, the United States became increasingly interested in Africa. Taken together, European and American ties (the former far more important than the latter by the tests of volume or quantity) with Africa form a dense network. Over 90 per cent of Africa's trade is with the West, and Western countries are overwhelmingly predominant as sources of public and private investment in Africa. Despite the expansion of African trade with the Communist countries in recent years, the great market for African products is still the West, and the Western countries are by far Africa's largest suppliers of manufactured goods and the "technical relationships" that go with them. Even the African military establishments—the archsymbols of sovereignty—have close ties with the West. Most African armies use Western equipment, and most senior officers and many junior personnel were trained in Western military schools. Western officers serve in some African armies, on secondment or as contract personnel.

Africa's cultural and educational ties are still predominantly with Western Europe. There are some 7,000 African students in the United States, perhaps an equal number in the Communist countries. But the combined figure is still far short of the 30,000–40,000 Africans studying in West European countries. Furthermore, the educational systems of most African countries have been adapted from a European base, and European teachers still play an important role in them. Finally—and it is hard to conceive of a cultural influence more important than this—English and French are both the "modern" and the common languages of Africa.

But for all the importance of these residual relationships, there are uncertainties concerning the future of Western political influence in Africa. Doubtless, it is declining and will continue to do so. What are uncertain are the level at which it will be stabilized and the intervening events that will help to determine what the level will be.

The West's relationships with Africa as a determinant of African foreign policies

Africa reacts to images of the West as a whole as well as to individual Western countries. These images were formed during the colonial period, which, for many Africans, has not yet come to an end. The West has provided the most visible external elements in African life and the elements most logically connected with the problems Africa has inherited. Therefore, Africa's attempts to shake itself loose from these problems must involve, by their very nature, a weakening of ties with the West.

1. *Neutralism*. African neutralism is, historically, a reaction against the West. As the African countries have become independent, they have in effect served notice that they were moving out of the Western state system and that, whatever ties they might retain, they were not to be expected to align themselves automatically with the West on international questions. Put in another way, Africa's leaders have made clear that, whatever they inherited from the West, they did not want to inherit any international commitments.

2. *Institutional successors to the colonial tie*. Neutralism has been complicated by the fact that various institutional successors to the colonial tie are of considerable value to African countries. The Commonwealth, the sterling area, the franc zone, the European Economic Community are all "institutions" to which various African countries belong by virtue of having been European colonies. To some degree, all these groupings orient African countries toward the West, but their effectiveness in this respect should not be exaggerated. Both Ghana and Nigeria, for example, are members of the Commonwealth; both Mali and Senegal are associates

of the EEC. In and of themselves, these ties do not limit the freedom of African countries to do what they please. But they must be taken into account by any African country in framing its foreign policy, since, together with the important "noninstitutionalized" ties with the former metropoles, they provide substantial benefits to the African partners.

3. *Anticolonialism.* Often, the true degree of dependence on the former colonial power is exposed only after independence, and it is the resultant awareness that makes the idea of neocolonialism credible to Africans. Thus, after independence, a number of African countries, and not exclusively those commonly designated as "radical" states, continue to regard the former metropole as the enemy. Often, the United States, as the conspicuous ally of Europe, tends to be regarded as the greatest neocolonialist nation. This widespread concern over neocolonialism will almost certainly be a preoccupation of the upcoming political generation in Africa.

There are, of course, conventional colonial problems left to Africa (using the term "colonial" as a convenient shorthand for the Portuguese dependencies and the settler areas of the southern third of the continent). African leaders believe that the West has the power to solve these problems, i.e., to end white supremacist policies and bring African majority rule to Southern Africa. As long as the present Southern African regimes exist, therefore, they are likely to be major irritants in the relations between Africa and the West. The chances are, indeed, that they will become greater irritants as time goes by. This complex of problems is particularly significant because if there is any issue on which there is real consensus among African governments, it is that of Southern Africa. How the West responds to this concern, therefore, may well be the single most important determinant of its relations with Africa in the measurable future.

4. *African unity and intra-African relations.* It is partly the continuing African concern over the real and supposed legacies of the colonial relationship that makes the West an important element in intra-African relations. Those African leaders who have been in the forefront of efforts to create a supranational political unity in Africa have cited among their main arguments the vulnerability of Africa's weak states to manipulation by outside

powers and the advantages of strength through unity. Almost invariably, the outside powers referred to in this context are the Western countries. It would be incorrect to suppose that "Pan-Africanism" is nothing more than a reaction to the West. But certainly the idea of regulating the access of outside powers to the African continent has been a major element in the history of the various attempts to form an intra-African organization and, again, the outside powers most vividly in mind on such occasions are usually Western countries. A case in point is the Congo: From mid–1960 to the present, one of the main themes running through the efforts to form an intra-African organization has been the massive peace-keeping problem known as the Congo. A touchstone of all these efforts has been the role played by Western powers in the Congo, and the contrasting attitudes of African states toward the Congo question have played a major role in the efforts to develop an African state system.

The principal Western powers and their impact on African foreign policies

1. *France.* France is the Western power that retains the most intimate ties with Africa—a web of relationships so intricate that it is difficult to analyze. Through trade and financial arrangements, the former French African dependencies are linked to the franc zone, the French economy, and the EEC. France has been one of Africa's greatest single sources of economic aid, investment, military aid, and technical assistance. (Since Africanization has proceeded more slowly in former French than in former British dependencies, the importance of technical aid is correspondingly greater.) Cultural bonds with the former metropole seem to be particularly enduring, perhaps because there is a self-conscious character about French culture, which seems to compel a peculiarly intense commitment. Finally, one might suggest that there is something in President de Gaulle's political style that seems to exert a particularly strong influence on the ties between France and its former African colonies.

The pattern of French influence is by no means uniform. French influence in North Africa, although important, has been declining, and other non-African states have played a substantial role—the

United States in Morocco and Tunisia, the U.S.S.R. and perhaps other Communist countries in Algeria. But in sub-Saharan Africa —leaving aside as special (though not necessarily contradictory) cases Guinea, Mali, and now Congo (Brazzaville)—the intimacy of the relationship with France is quite extraordinary.

A main reason has been that France has done so much to meet the needs of those countries. This has reduced the temptation, strong in so many other African states, to pursue a policy of diversification, since there has been reason to doubt that any other outside country, or combination of countries, would be prepared to take on French commitments in economic and military aid, trade, technical assistance, and the educational and cultural field.

Perhaps the main result of the orientation toward Paris has been a reinforcement of the tendency of French-speaking sub-Saharan states to think of themselves as having a community of interests not shared by other African countries. They tend to look inward and think primarily in terms of relationships among themselves, rather than in terms of African continental politics.

French-speaking sub-Saharan Africa has its own background of unity, stemming from the interterritorial basis on which the nationalist movement developed, the existence of the West and Equatorial African federations in the colonial period, and the former common meeting ground of the metropole's political life. All these have contributed to the tendency of the French-speaking African states to act as a bloc in African politics.

The various institutional expressions of the relationship—UAM, UAMCE, OCAM—have also to some degree reflected French interests. Given the persistence of the idea of unity among these states, it was far better from the French point of view to encourage formalized ties than to discourage, much less oppose, them. Furthermore, in terms of long-range French interests, there was far more point in encouraging these countries to come together on the basis of their common inheritance from France than to try to exert influence in detail on the foreign policies of more than a dozen independent states.

The advantages of these arrangements to the African states involved have already been mentioned. The disadvantage has been that the former French states have been somewhat isolated from wider African concerns and that greater emphasis has been given to "bloc" politics in intra-African relations.

Another current in French policy toward Africa has become especially apparent in the last year or two. As the Western alliance has become looser and President de Gaulle has moved to assert a separate French role in the world (especially one separate from the United States) France has shown a marked willingness to work with—or accommodate itself to—radical, neutralist regimes. Algeria has been the touchstone of this policy, which presumably reflects a judgment in Paris that one of the ways in which an "independent" French role can be asserted is by winning the confidence of the "third world." This means a somewhat more relaxed French attitude toward changes in African regimes, and confidence in an ability to work with their successors. Presumably, Paris believes that, in the longer run, common Franco-African interests will preserve much of the intimacy of the present relationship, even though the forms may be altered. A more immediate result may be somewhat more "activist" foreign policies on the part of some former French dependencies, and their adherence in at least some degree to more "neutralist" positions.

2. *Great Britain.* In many respects, the French role in Africa is clear-cut and substantial. The British role is more diffuse and harder to pin down. Although the United Kingdom has relationships of substantial importance with its former dependencies, somehow their nature differs considerably from that between France and its former African territories. Perhaps the greatest difference lies in the fact that there have been severe economic limitations on the burdens that the U.K. could assume in postindependence Africa. Great Britain has had to be highly selective in its allocation of resources and, wherever possible, has sought to curtail, or at least not to expand, its governmental commitments.

The Commonwealth is important, of course, and there is perhaps a tendency to underrate it. From the African point of view, it has some utility as a pressure group, which can be used to influence the older members on questions of interest to the underdeveloped, newer members. On matters relating to South Africa and Rhodesia, the symbolic importance of attitudes expressed by and through the Commonwealth has been considerable. The Commonwealth is probably less important as an instrument for influencing African foreign policies except, perhaps, in the indirect sense that it provides a privileged forum and channel for the exchange of views.

By and large, British policy seems to have operated on the premise that the West African territories can handle themselves. East and Central Africa have been areas of greater concern. Here, Great Britain has been somewhat more willing to assume commitments (as witness her dispatch of troops after the January, 1964, army mutinies in Kenya, Uganda, and Tanganyika). But even so, there appear to be marked limits, and certainly with the decline of British strategic interest in East Africa, the limits have become progressively narrower. The self-imposed restraints on Britain's role raise major uncertainties concerning the future course of events in East and Central Africa. In a sense, the vacuum created by Britain's reduced role in those areas has not yet been filled.

Over the near term, Great Britain perhaps will have her greatest effect on African foreign policies through the problems of Southern Africa. Rhodesia is clearly a British concern, as the African countries have repeatedly reminded London, and African pressures have been a major consideration in Britain's response to the unilateral declaration of independence by the white minority government. The nature of British action in this situation—and African judgments of its effectiveness—will have a considerable bearing on how African states themselves react to the Rhodesian problem and may well have broader implications for the African image of the West. African governments tend to regard South Africa also as a British problem, in the sense that the United Kingdom (together with the United States) is considered to have sufficient economic power to force internal changes. This belief, together with Britain's responsibilities in the three former High Commission Territories, will probably make Great Britain a continuing target of African pressures on Southern African questions.

3. *The United States.* The U.S. role as a "superpower" exerting a major influence on the international environment is obvious. In this generalized sense, the United States is naturally a major influence on the foreign relations of the African states. But at the level of more specific and direct African interests, there is room for

doubt as to the importance of the United States as a major and immediate determinant of African foreign policies on issues of substantial and continuing concern to the African states.

Perhaps the first limitation on American influence is that the United States has not clearly assumed a major role in Africa. U.S. material—i.e., economic and military strategic—interests there are far less important than comparable U.S. interests in other major areas of the world. There have thus been serious reasons for the United States to limit its commitments and involvements in Africa. Reinforcing this has been a half-submerged assumption of U.S. policy—a reluctance to become involved in Africa in ways that could stimulate the more dangerous forms of Cold War rivalry— because of the belief (probably well-founded) that there was more to be lost than gained by inviting East-West confrontations in Africa.

In response both to these concerns and to the burden of other commitments, the United States has not attempted to replace the input or the influence of the former colonial powers. The U.S. presence in many African countries is minimal; in those countries where the presence is substantial—e.g., where the United States has entered into important economic aid commitments—there have been distinct limitations on U.S. political leverage.

Another limitation on American influence has been the diffi-culty that the United States has had in differentiating its role in Africa from that of the colonial powers. There is an irony in this, since a decade ago there were high American hopes that the United States would be regarded as standing for something dif-ferent—and desirable—in Africa. But the United States has not been able to—and probably could not—divorce its image in Africa from its image as the leader of the Western alliance, and it is too much to expect that Washington can view its role in Africa alto-gether in isolation from its world-wide commitments. Related is the fact that many U.S. concerns arising from this world-wide role are simply not credible to many Africans, who are preoccu-pied with different problems judged according to different cri-teria. Perhaps the best example—and an occasion on which the United States was indeed a major determinant of African foreign policies—has been the troublesome U.S. involvement in the Congo which was premised on concerns which—whether one agreed with them or not—were genuinely felt in Washington and were not at all persuasive to a number of African governments. The paradoxical result is that the United States seems to have had its main impact on the foreign policies of the radical or "revisionist" states. For many of them, the United States represents the resurgence of Western power in Africa, and U.S. policy—quite unintentionally—has increased their apprehensions and brought them closer together.

Because of U.S. reluctance to become too deeply involved in Africa, "gradual change" and such related concepts as "peace-keeping" have been recurrent themes of U.S. policy in Africa. For some African governments, these are simply expressions of an effort to preserve the *status quo*.

The Congo has been an area where U.S. policy, seen in this light, has attracted the opposition of Africa's "activist" states. The same kind of pressures will increasingly be exerted with respect to U.S. policy in the southern third of the continent, on which the lines of African differences are less sharply drawn than they have been in the case of the Congo, and where the United States, like Britain, is regarded, rightly or wrongly, as holding a key to the solution.

THE COMMUNIST WORLD AND AFRICA

The Rise of the Communist world and the end of the colonial system

The withdrawal of Western power from Africa and Asia has roughly coincided with the emergence of the Communist world's challenge to the power of the West. The expansion of the Soviet Union after World War II, and the concomitant rise of Communist China, had no direct connection with the "African revolution." But the existence of the "socialist camp" has been a major determinant of the international environment into which the African states have been born. The Communist state system is a source of pressure on the West which makes the West a good deal more responsive to African needs, a force trying to propel Africa out of isolation and into the mainstream of international politics, and a major power center (now really two power centers) trying to attract Africa into its orbit. Above all, the Communist world has been able to identify itself with change in Africa in a way the West could not. The Sino-Soviet states have had thus far no divided sense of responsibility, no "presence" in the Western sense, to preserve. None of this predisposes African states to be any less jealous of their independence, but it certainly does not prejudice them against the "socialist camp."

The Communist world's policies in Africa

Setting aside the question of long-range goals, one can compress the Communist world's present policies into the following categories:

1. *To gain access.* Until the "independence explosion," Africa was, with few exceptions, a denied area to the Communist countries. State-to-state relations were obviously not possible, and Communist parties were of minor importance, except perhaps in Algeria and South Africa. The first objective of the Communist states, therefore, has been to establish access to Africa through the usual governmental instrumentalities—diplomatic relations, economic, technical, and military aid—and through expanded contacts with groups such as political parties, trade unions, and youth organizations. The second category of relationships has involved not only bilateral contacts but also the traditional Communist international front organizations and a new type of "Afro-Asian" organization uniting Communist and radical nationalist elements, such as the Afro-Asian Peoples Solidarity Organization (AAPSO).

2. *To reduce and, if possible, to eliminate Western influence in Africa.* With its access to the continent widening, the Communist world's immediate policy goal is to weaken and, if possible, liquidate the Western position there. Since this objective is shared by many African countries, it establishes a certain congruence of goals between them and the Communist states from the very beginning. Perhaps only a few African leaders would agree that Western influence should be eliminated altogether, but there are many who would regard a weakening of residual Western influence as desirable.

The African preoccupation with "neocolonialism"—the shorthand term for the persistence of the Western presence after independence—did not originate in Communist influence. This concern is an almost predictable reaction to postindependence conditions: The ending of the colonial tie exposes the almost intolerable weaknesses of the new states, since the underpinnings of the colonial relationship cannot be altered by a mere change in sovereignty. The battle against "colonialism" therefore continues in a new form.

3. *To promote an identity of interests between the Communist states and Africa in international affairs.* Beyond fostering a common interest in curtailing Western power in Africa, the Communist countries seek to promote a more general alliance between themselves and the newly independent states. To that end, they press the concept of a community of interests between the "socialist camp" and the underdeveloped world, with the "imperialist" countries as a common antagonist. There are real differences between the U.S.S.R. and Communist China about the immediate objectives of this alliance—e.g., as between "peace" and "liberation"— but the differences should not be exaggerated. Both major Communist powers are concerned to link the emergent African states to the "socialist camp."

4. *To encourage the radicalization of African regimes.* Africa presents difficult doctrinal problems for Moscow and Peking, but has also helped to foster a new flexibility in their tactics. Traditional Marxist-Leninist schema seemed to set far distant goals when applied to the African *milieu*. Furthermore, in most African countries, Communist parties did not exist even in embryo. But the radical, modernizing regimes in some African states seem to resemble Communist regimes in sentiment, method, and aspiration. For the present, therefore, the Communists have muted their old animosity to revolutionary ideologies that do not conform to their own doctrine and control. The "national democracies," now styled "revolutionary democracies," are presumed to be moving toward orthodox Communism. The Communist world sees its task as one of guarding, aiding, encouraging those regimes, with a view ultimately to drawing them into its own orbit. Seen from Moscow or Peking, the process must be fraught with many uncertainties. How long will it take? The process is "natural" and "inevitable,"

but will external Communist intervention be required at some stage? Can one be certain the process will not go awry, leaving political doctrines competitive with Communism entrenched in Africa's most "activist" states? At this time, however, the Russians and Chinese perhaps do not have to face these problems. The indicators seem to point toward more Malis, Guineas, Congos (Brazzaville). But with the pattern of African politics so new, there must be persistent uncertainties.

The Communist world as a determinant of African foreign policies

1. *An alternative to dependence on the West.* The Communist world offers Africa an alternative and counterweight to the West. Both major Communist powers must limit their involvements in Africa; their commitments to date have been far less than those of the West, but they have been substantial. No African government, presumably, wishes to exchange total dependence on a Western country for total dependence on a Communist country. The prospect of "diversification," however, makes African foreign policies more independent (and, on occasion, more adventurous) and provides African states with an important source of leverage in their relations with Western countries.

Limitations on this leverage stem from the fact that, like everyone else, the Communist countries have no magic keys to economic development and have limited resources. As far as Africa is concerned, therefore, the Communist states are not altogether satisfactory alternatives to the West. But the problem of an "exchange of dependence" (a "pre-emptive" situation, as the outsider would see it) hardly ever arises. From the Africans' point of view, the trick is to keep both sides interested, to encourage them to measure their own influence by the extent to which they remain competitive with each other, and to yield as little as possible in return.

2. *The Communist world and the "anti-imperialist front."* Both the Russians and the Chinese have sought, with some success, to ally themselves to the African countries on issues of major concern to Africans. In a sense, the Russians and Chinese have enlisted themselves in various African causes—e.g., the campaign

against white minority control in Southern Africa; Pan-Africanism; the "struggle against neocolonialism"—because those causes serve Communist world objectives against the West and identification with them serves as a "transmission belt" for Communist influence in Africa. The immediate goal of Moscow and Peking is to link African countries with an "anti-imperialist" front, and to broaden African concerns to include non-African issues important to the Communist states.

As a result of this process, African issues and concerns are magnified and projected, and their impact on world affairs is intensified. The Congo's importance as an international issue, for example, has been enhanced by the role that Communist countries —especially the Soviet Union—have played in respect to the Congo at various times. Sino-Soviet involvement in African issues also has encouraged the coalescence of blocs in Africa. Just as some states have found common ground in, *inter alia*, their receptivity to a working relationship with the Communist world, others have been drawn together in part by misgivings over the expansion of Communist influence. There is a difference between Soviet and U.S. policies in this respect. The Russians feel they have more to gain from such a division in Africa, since they are convinced that the radical, revisionist states are the wave of the future and that others will join them in due course. American policy is more cautious. One suspects that the United States would prefer greater African unity (or less disunity) within a more strictly defined framework of neutralism.

3. *The Communist world and "revisionist" politics in Africa.* The Communist world has achieved its greatest success in Africa by attracting countries whose general outlook is radical and "revisionist," i.e., which seek fundamental changes in the relationship between Africa and the outside world and, related to this, fundamental changes within Africa as well. They are the states conventionally known as "radicals"—a somewhat elastic category embracing a variety of differences. Usually listed as "hard-core radicals" are Algeria, the U.A.R., Ghana, Guinea, Mali, and Congo (Brazzaville). But other states sometimes cooperate with that group, without, so to speak, taking out, or even qualifying for, membership: Kenya, Uganda, Sudan, and Tanzania are recent

examples. The pattern and criteria of African radicalism become even more blurred when one recalls, for example, that Morocco, a conservative state in all essentials, was once a member of the Casablanca Group and that Somalia, while greatly dependent on the U.S.S.R. for aid, has lacked a number of characteristics commonly associated with radical states.

For reasons of their own, the radical states are willing to accept close and even intimate ties with the U.S.S.R. and Communist China. None of them even approaches a complete dependence on the Communist world; on the contrary, all of them have vital links with Western countries. But in a variety of ways, the radical states tend to accept a harmony of interest with the "socialist camp" which they do not share with the West.

The policies of the radical states are in many respects congruent with those of the Communist countries, not only on African issues but on broader international questions as well. In general, the radicals' preoccupations are with ridding Africa of the vestiges of white domination, with curtailing Western influence on the continent, with constructing an intra-African system strong enough to gain those goals, and, to all of these ends, with encouraging the development of regimes having a similar orientation. In these enterprises, they see the Communist countries as useful allies.

This relationship has not compromised the independence or freedom of action of the states involved. One should bear in mind that the leaders of the radical countries are among the toughest-minded in Africa. Furthermore, both the Russians and Chinese generally have sought to avoid heavy-handedness (not always successfully) and temptations to press for too much too soon. The attraction to date has been voluntary or "consensual," and to both Moscow and Peking, it is the hopeful trend in Africa.

4. *The Sino-Soviet split: a new determinant of African foreign policies?* The U.S.S.R. and Communist China obviously have many objectives in common in Africa. But they are also competitors for power, both in the international community of states and in the international Communist movement. Although Africa has not been a major arena of Sino-Soviet competition, there have been unmistakable signs of rivalry and there will probably be more rather than less in the future. For one thing, the under-

developed areas are crucial to the Sino-Soviet controversy, since one of its main themes is the proper place of the "third world" in Communist strategy.

How does this conflict—one of the most significant of the modern era—affect the foreign policies of the African states? Presumably no African state wants to choose sides between Moscow and Peking. But at the same time, the Sino-Soviet conflict is not without advantages from the African point of view. For one thing, just as Cold War rivalries give African governments additional leverage in their relations with both East and West, so the Sino-Soviet rivalry gives them additional possibilities of leverage in their relations with Communist states. African governments presumably can profit to the extent that both the U.S.S.R. and Communist China bid against each other for African favors. Furthermore, to the extent that the Communist world loses its monolithic character, African governments will assume that they have less to fear from it, for not only does the West exist as a balance but there are now counterweights within the Communist system as well. For some African states, this fear may never have existed, but for others the Sino-Soviet conflict may remove a restraint on dealing with the Communist world.

Finally, the Sino-Soviet conflict may affect the style and content of African "neutralism." Moscow and Peking seem to encourage somewhat different kinds of neutralism. The Soviet Union appears to envisage a gradual alignment of third-world countries with the socialist camp, leading ultimately to a shrinkage and constraint of Western power and to a fundamental shift in the world balance of forces, all without provoking a major confrontation between the West and the Communist world. The Chinese, however, project an aggressive neutralism, involving constant pressure and even provocation against the West, and especially against the United States, on the theory (somewhat contradictory, to be sure) that the West will retreat before those challenges or, if it does not, will solidify the third world even more solidly against it by an aggressive response.

This is not to say that either the Soviet or Chinese brand of neutralism will necessarily win the allegiance of Africa, for African countries have their own conceptions of self-interest. But the

African states will nonetheless find themselves subject to pressures from each major Communist power center to make their policies conform to one or the other of the types of neutralism, and the pressures are likely to grow stronger over the forseeable future.

The U.N., the Afro-Asian "Bloc," and Africa

Although the U.N. and the Afro-Asian "bloc" are two dissimilar categories (and the latter term requires considerable explanation and qualification), they have, for Africa, an essential attribute in common: Both are means of expressing what might be called "organized neutralism" and of magnifying and projecting African influence on international affairs. They are determinants of African foreign policy in another sense than that in which the countries of the West or the Communist world are determinants. Africa tends to react to the latter, to be compelled by historical circumstances to establish a relationship with them, whether it wishes to or not. But the U.N. and the various groupings of Afro-Asian states are determinants first and foremost because they offer instrumentalities and forums for the assertion and enhancement of African interests. That they are also channels for pressures to which African countries must respond is perhaps of secondary importance.

The United Nations

1. *U.N. membership as "accreditation."* The initial, historical impact of the U.N. on African foreign policies was fairly simple but important. Membership in the U.N. provided "accreditation" for newly independent states, a symbolic and collective recognition by the international political community that they were indeed sovereign and independent. Furthermore, U.N. membership was also to some extent a guarantee of the new states, not in any strict sense, but at least in the sense that admission signified that the new states had a "right to exist" and that the international community could not be completely oblivious to their fate.

2. *The U.N. as a forum for exerting African influence.* Perhaps even more important, the U.N. has been a forum for exerting African influence on the international community and particularly

on the great powers. As the number of independent African states has multiplied, so African representation in the U.N. has increased to the point where African countries now account for almost one-third of its membership. While it would be inaccurate to suggest that an African bloc exists in the U.N., there is certainly an "African interest" that transcends to some degree interstate rivalries, and the African delegations are recognized as forming a distinct grouping or caucus (this has been formalized in part as a result of the historic role of the African U.N. delegations as a mechanism for urgent consultations among the African states and for continuing contact in the intervals between intra-African conferences).

Related to the growth of African representation have been the recent attempts to expand and "institutionalize" third-world interests in the U.N., a reflection of the concern shared by many African, Asian, and Latin American countries that the significant division in the U.N. is not between East and West but between the great powers and other developed states on one hand and the underdeveloped areas on the other. One aspect of this has been the effort to expand African membership in the U.N. councils. Another has been the creation of what may prove to be a major new body within the U.N. framework, the Trade and Development Board—an outgrowth of the United Nations Conference on Trade and Development (UNCTAD)—to serve as a continuing body for the discussion of economic issues between the developed and underdeveloped countries.

The U.N. has traditionally been a place where African states have sought to mobilize interest in and support for African goals which they have been unable to achieve unaided. The U.N.'s historic function in African eyes has been as a generator of pressures for decolonization, and this role has continued unabated from the early days of the Trusteeship Council to the present-day Committee of Twenty-four. The emphasis now, of course, is on Southern Africa, and in a variety of ways the U.N. provides a means of inducing, persuading, or even compelling other states to assist in the task which African countries still lack the material power to accomplish by themselves—the elimination of the white regimes of Southern Africa.

3. *The U.N. as an intervener in African affairs.* The U.N. has also acted in another way as a determinant of African foreign policies, in its capacity as an intervener in African affairs. In point of fact, there has been only one clear-cut case, the Congo intervention of 1960–64, but that single instance seems to have been enough to fix or at least strongly influence African attitudes toward this kind of U.N. activity.

During the tense—and in the Congo, chaotic—days of 1960 and 1961, there was no consensus within the U.N. on what ought to be done (other than "something"), and as a consequence the U.N. Secretary General was both freer—and perhaps under a more definite obligation—to take initiatives. The Congo had become a cockpit of intra-African politics, and in deciding to treat with this or that authority in Leopoldville, or to take or refrain from taking a given action in, say, the Katanga, the U.N. necessarily had to cut across lines of African interest. That was no doubt all the more galling to some African governments because of the presence of African military contingents in the U.N. force in the Congo (UNOC), which were only partially responsive to their home governments. Finally, the U.N. action was interpreted in some quarters as a screen for great-power intervention. Although one might add parenthetically that this view was greatly oversimplified, the U.N. operation in the Congo certainly involved the major powers in a way that split across the conventional East-West divisions. The United States supported U.N. involvement in the Congo and provided substantial logistical support for UNOC. The U.S.S.R. was opposed to the U.N. role, and, especially as the problem of Katangan reintegration loomed larger and larger, both Britain and France showed in practice a closer affinity for the Soviet than for the U.S. position. Nonetheless, U.N. involvement in the Congo could not help drawing the great powers into the Congo's problems in some way.

The Congo situation crystallized already latent divisions among the newly independent African countries, and it could be said that the points of crystallization were various acts of commission and omission by the U.N. in and concerning the Congo. The divisions between the Casablanca and the Monrovia/Lagos groups were, historically speaking, divisions over the Congo situation and the U.N.'s involvement therein.

Since the Congo experience, African attitudes toward the U.N. can perhaps best be described as ambiguous. Despite the usual shadings of their individual positions, African states generally are somewhat wary about the U.N., and desire to exercise a veto over U.N. action in Africa. They proceed from a belief both that U.N. involvement injects non-African elements into African problems and, conversely, that such problems can best be solved within the African community of states. In attempting to establish common institutions for an African state system, at least some African countries seem to have had in mind an arrangement under which the African states, through their joint organization, would act as the "agent" for the U.N. in dealing with problems and conflicts arising within the African state system.

The Afro-Asian bloc and African foreign policies

1. *Does it exist?* In a strict sense, of course, there is no such thing as an Afro-Asian bloc. The almost bewildering heterogeneity of the Afro-Asian world, the great variety of conflicts within it—not only conflicts of interest but shooting wars or near-shooting wars as well—all attest to the impossibility of speaking of the Afro-Asian countries as a political entity.

Granted all these incompatibilities, there is still a rudimentary sense of common interests among the Afro-Asian states, deriving from common political styles and problems, from common concerns for development and the restructuring of the world economy, and from what might be called a community of negative interests. These are interests *against* the West for the most part, since practically all Afro-Asian countries are still reacting to the colonial period as they try to find and assert their own identities. Their community of interests has found political expression in various loose associations, often identified with a particular conference, e.g., Belgrade or Bandung.

2. *Afro-Asian politics as a determinant of African foreign policies.* Africa's involvement in Afro-Asian politics is held within certain limits by the inward-looking character of the African states. Through their participation in such forums as the U.N., the Belgrade (1961) and Cairo (1964) conferences of "nonaligned countries," and UNCTAD and its successor, the U.N. Trade and Development Board, at least some African countries have become

increasingly aware that they share aims and political attitudes with the Arab and Asian countries. The most obvious effect of this in the case of Afro-Asian groupings is that Africans—like the other participants—gain another platform for projecting their views, one that is more under their own control than are the U.N. or its subordinate bodies. In many ways, the various Afro-Asian bodies and conferences are pressure groups, whose purpose is to impress upon the Eastern and Western countries the need to take into account African and Asian goals and points of view. Functioning in this capacity, Afro-Asian groupings have sometimes provided an opportunity for individual African states to play a greater, or at least more prominent, role in world affairs than is usually the case when they operate from within a purely African framework. Thus, for a time, Algeria took on a new importance in international politics through its role, together with China and Indonesia, in organizing the aborted "second Bandung" conference; Mali's stature was enhanced when President Keita acted as one of the formal bearers of the resolutions of the 1961 Belgrade conference to Washington; and Kenya's significance in international affairs was greater as a signatory to the Yugoslav-sponsored (but largely Afro-Asian) seventeen-country appeal on Viet-Nam of March, 1965.

Those efforts all tend to fall in the category of what might be called "organized neutralism"; i.e., they represent collective efforts by African and Asian states to exert more influence on the international environment. At the same time, they have certain other effects that are perhaps less welcome to many African countries.

First, they tend to draw African states—quite unwillingly, for the most part—into extra-African problems. The Arab-Israeli problem is an example, deriving in the first instance from the fact that the African state system includes several Arab countries. In Afro-Asian political forums, Black African states sometimes find themselves in embarrassing situations as a result of attempts to involve them in the Arab-Israeli dispute, since on those occasions the Arab states usually try to commit the participants to a strongly worded and widely publicized denunciation of Israel. There are other examples as well—Kashmir, Cyprus, Malaysia—and the number is likely to increase as times goes on.

Second, and ironically, the various efforts at organized Afro-Asian neutralism sometimes involve Africans more deeply in what they presumably are trying to avoid—great-power politics, including East-West tensions and the Sino-Soviet conflict.

The efforts of organized neutralism, as distinct from the policies of individual countries, by their nature tend to be directed against the West. The Communist countries have therefore sought to associate themselves with these movements, even though they may create future problems for the Communist world. Thus, at the October, 1964, "nonaligned conference" in Cairo—the successor to the 1961 Belgrade meeting—the Soviet Union was able to identify itself with the "middle-of-the-road" position, as against the United States on one side and Communist China on the other. As long as there is no *rapprochement* between Moscow and Peking, it is possible that the U.S.S.R. will be able to perpetuate this identification and that a Soviet-sponsored nonalignment will be credible to some African countries.

For some of the activist African states, nonalignment, even according to the style of the Belgrade group, is too passive a concept. There is more appeal in the Communist Chinese efforts to organize an Afro-Asian "anti-imperialist front," manifested in 1965 in the unsuccessful attempt to convene a second Bandung conference. This front would not be a nonaligned group in any meaningful sense of the word, but rather a coalition of aggressive, activist African and Asian countries seeking to act as a cohesive group in international affairs, perhaps even associating themselves with the vague Indonesian proposals to form a "replacement" for the U.N. Such a grouping would of course be strongly anti-Western. It would also be at least implicitly anti-Soviet, since it would represent an extension of Chinese influence in Africa and Asia and would permit Peking to claim—with some justification—that it is the center of the community of anti-imperialist states.

With all of this said about the external political determinants of African foreign policies, some caveats are in order. First of all, there is that dangerous term "Africa." There are, of course, many Africas, including some three dozen independent states, each with its own distinctive character and history, and each pursuing its own conception of national interest. The terms "Africa" and "African" have been freely and deliberately used in the foregoing, since the intention has been to extract the general from the particular. But the generalizations have been made with full awareness that they necessarily sacrifice a level of accuracy and qualification—that of the particular and the unique.

Furthermore, when the external political influences on Africa are catalogued, the inadequacy of such a treatment is immediately evident. In the modern world of interdependence, relationships proliferate in intricate webs, and all influences are somehow interrelated. In some respects, it is artificial to separate one category under the rubric "external political determinants." Political relationships are a summing up of all relationships, and much goes into them that is not political in the narrow sense. To take a fundamental example, the Western cultural relationship with Africa—considering this relationship in its broadest meaning—is the matrix of Western political ties and thus, in a sense, a "determinant of the determinants." To take another example, a treatment on this scale can do no more than suggest some of the technological factors in external political influence.

Like any other analysis, the analysis of external political influences on African regimes requires that the process which is being studied be stopped in midpassage, so that it can be weighed and measured. One must generalize from a static model about situations that are continually evolving. In the case of Africa, the difficulty is compounded by our lack of historical perspective. So many things are happening on the continent for the first time that conclusions must be tentative. One must be careful, therefore, not to judge still malleable patterns as if they were fixed.

Finally, this chapter is limited to the outside world's political influence on Africa. One must keep in mind, however, that the existence of an influence or determinant creates a relationship and that relationships, by definition, are reciprocal. Although the outside world is the stronger partner in relationships with Africa, it is still a partner. Africa is also a determinant of the foreign policies of non-African countries. Its emergence has altered the calculus of world politics by introducing a new set of elements—and a new range of risks, complications, and opportunities. Africa is something to which the outside world must respond, in one way or another, and it is therefore an agent as well as an object of influence in international relations.

VIII

Research Needs

VERNON McKAY

Many stimulating suggestions for further research on African international relations were made during the symposium discussion of the foregoing chapters. Moreover, a final session was devoted specifically to the consideration of further research subjects, methods, and approaches. While it is neither desirable nor feasible to publish a complete report of the discussion, it seems worth while to summarize the numerous suggestions for additional research. In addition to the ideas presented by the two commentators who initiated the discussion of each paper, the following synthesis incorporates suggestions by other participants, as well as written observations submitted after the meeting.

NATIONAL INTEREST AND IDEOLOGY

The discussion of national interest and ideology emphasized the need for more work on the subject if only to clarify the concepts and the problems it raised. Carl Rosberg and Ruth Schachter Morgenthau were the discussants for the Zartman paper. Rosberg questioned the usefulness of the distinction drawn between national interest and ideology. Although Zartman had recognized that most policies contain elements of both, he had nonetheless focused on the differences between national-interest (pragmatic or consociational) regimes, which concentrated on solving socio-economic problems, and ideological (revolutionary or mobilizational) regimes, which concentrated on the political problems stemming largely from the absence of strong and stable authority patterns. However, if it is true that interstate relationships are only of marginal importance in overcoming the fragility of the new African states, then there are major drawbacks to regarding the concepts of national interest and security as determinants of African foreign policies. In particular, the language of national-interest theory had emerged from the pattern of interstate relations among Western powers in which "national security" had more explicit meanings. The German concept of Realpolitik related mainly to the attempts of European powers to strengthen their security against external aggression, but in Africa, as Zartman had noted, external aggression is only a minor problem.

Although he recognized Zartman's valuable contribution in pointing out the "consolidation, identification, and assurance" functions of ideology in African foreign policies, Rosberg felt that Zartman's approach tended to disguise certain ethnocentric Western assumptions. Rosberg suggested that a more meaningful method of examining African foreign policies would be to study the kinds of assaults that are made by African leaders on the existing interstate system, and the significance of such attacks for foreign policy.

Ruth Morgenthau remarked that the relationship between ideas and reality plagues all human life, of man with himself and man with others; it touches on the connections between the inside and outside world and between the spheres of Freud and Marx, who never did make peace with each other. No wonder that so many problems arise from the perceptions and actions of African leaders when confronted with the new realities of international life. Stressing that foreign relations is not an independent variable but a subsidiary of internal, domestic considerations, Professor Morgenthau asked whether ideology is a "screen" for reality or "a guide to action within reality." If it is a screen to hide reality, its adoption may mean national suicide. Ideology, she concluded, is not always an aberration; it can be a rational guide to action.

In the ensuing discussion, several participants expressed concern over the definition of concepts. Zartman had used the idea of national interest only as a territorial concept, but African national-ism also has an African or continental aspect. The example of Ghana's policy over the Congo or South Africa was cited as pos-sibly a national-interest policy and not an ideological policy, if one thought in terms of African nationalism rather than Ghanaian nationalism. Another participant found it difficult to follow the separation of ideas and interests in specific situations. He suggested that all states operate out of interest motives defined by a view of the world and by objectives that have ideological preconceptions. At different times, different aspects are stressed. A distinction was also drawn between national and "nonnational" interest. Most in-terests as defined by statesmen today are "transnational," because of the interaction of all states; in fact, no state operates solely according to the national interest. "We are all ruled by the bal-ance of terror," so that in a sense all Africans operate out of a sense of transnational interest. As expressed by another participant, terminological precision might suggest that the term *"national interest"* is not appropriate when one is dealing with countries which are not yet nations; or, to put the same point in a more concrete way, the conception of national goals by people in the process of creating national unity must surely be very different from the conception of such goals by people who believe that they have achieved national unity. There is considerable evidence on the African scene to show that the national interest of a state goes beyond its territorial boundaries and involves concern with Africa as a whole. But it goes even further than that. For many African leaders, national policy is motivated by a determination to give validity and significance to the role of the black man in the modern political world.

The term "ideology" in relation to African situations may also be misleading unless one is careful to bear in mind that in the new African states—to a greater degree than in the Western world—the ideology with which the state is labeled represents the ac-ceptance by the people of a doctrine offered by a charismatic leader, rather than the evolutionary adoption of a set of ideas produced in the course of the country's history.

The need to analyze the content of African ideologies was also emphasized. For example, further studies might be made of the ideology of *négritude*, of the philosophy of Islam in Africa, of President Nkrumah's consciencism, of African socialism, and of the ideology of apartheid. While some participants felt that documentation was too limited for certain types of content analysis, others felt that there were important possibilities in this field. A survey of the vernacular press using elements of content analysis was mentioned as a way of analyzing African conceptions and perceptions.

An African participant did not believe that foreign-policy decisions in Africa were clearly made according to either national-interest or ideological motives. Whatever the preliminary considerations, in the end the national interest had to be paramount in order to give any sense to the word "government." He regarded both the short history of African participation in world politics and the total of foreign-policy decisions thus far made as too limited for profound analysis.

He felt that not enough attention had been paid to what Africans say about nonalignment. When Africans say that it is their principal commitment, they mean it. In view of this fact, there is bound to be inconsistency and lack of pattern in decision-making, since every decision is made *ad hoc*.

He asked how the group would categorize Sierra Leone's decision to recognize Taiwan. It was not a national-interest policy, since it might result in Sierra Leone's not receiving aid from the Communist world. But it also couldn't be ideological, since Sierra Leone was committed to the admission of Mainland China to U.N. membership.

Zartman suggested that perhaps certain *principles* constitute another determinant in African decision-making. Principles, he thought, seemed to characterize Tunisia's foreign policy. When asked how a researcher might separate into "boxes" information on national-interest versus ideological determinants, Zartman replied that, because of their elusive character, he had deliberately avoided precise definition of his concepts. He thought, however, that actions could generally be "boxed" as one or the other depending on the motives and objectives given them. This would require a study of the process of decision-making as well as of the action itself. To assess their ideological bias, one would have to analyze the content of statements by the dominant elites, and try to find which actions were consistent with ideological statements.

Asked about the difference between an ideology and a simple value scheme, Zartman stated that he viewed ideology as more of a structure than a value. Ideology is the end of a gamut of values and principles that lead to a structured belief which is the ideology. Since it starts as an abstract concept but is later applied by foreign-policy makers, in a sense it is both a screen and a guide. It meets reality yet disregards some of the "law of things" because it wants to change those things.

Several speakers suggested the need for "attitude studies" in order to determine how elites actually perceive their goals, a matter of central concern in the understanding of foreign-policy formulation. How do Africans view their relations with their former metropoles—with the Cold War groupings to which they must relate; with each other; or with the Arab North? The differing perceptions of ethnic groups resulting from different traditional orientations and different opportunities are all related to foreign-policy attitudes.

A participant asked whether Africans' views of their own state system differ from their views of the international state system. Further study was needed of the conceptions that Africans have regarding their own relationships to the international state system. Another participant felt that this was the key question: Will Africans adapt to and accept the present international system, or will they seek to transform it?

An African participant expressed the view that the trouble with the UAM-OCAM grouping was that it attempted to structure Africa's international relations around a non-African factor, the French language. By 1980, he felt, such a factor, along with the common experiences of the first-generation African leaders, would have become less important. French-speaking African states would build their international relationships on new bases.

It was suggested that a useful series of studies might be made of African attitudes toward the West in general, and toward the Communist world, as well as toward specific countries outside Africa.

The problem of outsiders' attitudes toward Africa, also raised by several participants, in part reflected on the adequacy of Western-derived concepts as models for the study of the African state system. But it also raised the larger question of the need for studying bias and preconceptions in the outside world regarding African diplomacy.

ECONOMIC DETERMINANTS

Arnold Rivkin and Albert Tevoedjre were the two discussants for Andrew Kamarck's chapter on economic determinants. Remarking that "man does not live by manioc alone," Rivkin judged ideology to be an integral part of national interest. He shared Kamarck's view that the economic decisions of African leaders had thus far been quite impressive in their reasonableness. One could contend, for example, that it was the economic factor that influenced Morocco to keep United States military bases so long, rather than emphasize, as many observers did, that it was political or ideological factors that forced the United States to get out. It depends on how you look at it. African leaders do occasionally indulge in escapism because they come to independence heavily overcommitted with electoral promises and find their problems unsolvable, but on the whole their behavior has been remarkably rational.

Rivkin questioned Kamarck's suggestion that Africa is relatively unimportant to Europe economically. He pointed out that South Africa, for example, is very important to the United Kingdom and that trade with Morocco, Tunisia, Ivory Coast, Gabon, and Senegal are quite important to France.

Rivkin also questioned Kamarck's emphasis on customs unions and the resulting larger markets as a solution to current economic problems. He pointed out that African states such as Liberia, Sierra Leone, and Guinea, for example, are economic competitors in their exports, and he felt that Africa has a long way to go before its economies become sufficiently complementary to develop into a common market.

Both Rivkin and Tevoedjre questioned the view that the former French territories have consciously chosen to maintain their economic ties with France. Have they really had any choice? Tevoedjre also disagreed with Kamarck's thesis that the French-speaking states have benefited from their relationship with France. Their national budgets, in many cases, are substantially smaller than that of the Galeries Lafayette in Paris. Moreover, the economic dependence carried over from the colonial period puts an African in the position of an Alpinist who is thrown a rope that enables him to cling to a cliff, exhausted. The rope saves him from immediate death, but as long as he remains hanging in the air, he is at the mercy of the person holding the rope.

Tevoedjre cited the case of Dahomey as an illustration. It purchases 75 per cent *ad valorem* of its merchandise within the franc zone, and exports about 80 per cent of its products to France. When the world market for raw materials is at its worst point, France sustains Dahomey by purchasing Dahomey's palm oil at a price higher than the world market price. But France does so on condition that Dahomey buy its imports from French industry. In 1961, for example, Dahomey sold 68,131 tons of products to France for 2,581,809,000 francs CFA, but it purchased 76,921 tons of merchandise for 3,679,271,000 francs CFA.

The Dahomeyan deficit was therefore a daily specter, although France, with increasing difficulty, balanced Dahomey's administrative budget by grants of more than 3 billion francs CFA between 1960 and 1963. If French support had been suddenly removed, Dahomey would have collapsed overnight. Tevoedjre called this policy of chaining the client state to the protector's market the "sugar cube" policy. The client state becomes hypnotized by the lure of aid from the metropole, just as Pavlov's dogs were hypnotized by the sugar cube. But the client state is only given sufficient time to nibble a corner off the sugar cube, so that its hunger is not satisfied. Most aid is extended for a short term— one month, two months, six months at the maximum—and it's always insufficient to cover the needs of the particular period. The beggar is thus perpetually uncertain. Pulled into an almost scientifically refined combination, he is unceasingly obliged to solicit new credit and to be careful of any "imprudence" likely to annoy the protector. Tevoedjre suggested that the timidity of several of the French-speaking African states in adopting a pro-Algerian position during the Algerian conflict was clearly attributable to the sugar cube policy.

Tevoedjre pointed out that Dahomey had its own yams but imported French potatoes, as well as eggs, from Marseilles. Dahomeyans drive imported cars, wear imported clothes, smoke imported cigarettes, and drink imported whisky and wine. Until this stops, he concluded, and Dahomeyans learn to live on their own resources, they will have no independence, no nonalignment, and no foreign policy.

In the ensuing discussion, several participants stressed that no country today lives on its own resources. Kamarck felt that African states must have aid in the first stage in order to get the development process under way; therefore, it was not so bad to use imports bought with aid at this stage. Another participant suggested that perhaps African statesmen should follow the maxim "Never begin as a luxury what you can't continue as a habit."

A speaker pointed out that Africa's dependence on the West is further enhanced by the dependence of some international organizations on the West. The Soviet Union does not participate in the World Bank, IFC, IDA, IMF, and FAO, so that, if Western contributions to these organizations were smaller, there would be less opportunity for African participation, and international borrowing would presumably be reduced.

The interpretation of economic history as a determinant of behavior was also noted. The commonly presented picture of the metropolitan-colonial economic relationship as one of mutual exclusiveness is not only far too simple as a generalization, but, at least as far as the ex-British colonies are concerned, is generally false. Thus, there were French, Swiss, Dutch, German, Indian, and Levantine firms in the Gold Coast and Nigeria. The constituent firms of the Unilever group, which incidentally competed sharply with each other, were not restricted to buying and selling within the imperial connection.

Study is needed of how current political attitudes are affected by the way in which political leaders interpret the histories of their countries in relation to the colonial economic systems. A distinction should be made between what a colonial structure was in fact (whatever its imperfections—including those that we, with the benefits of hindsight and different political outlooks, attribute to it) and the distortions it could assume. The interpretation (or misinterpretation) of history can sometimes be a useful political tool. Is Nasser's statement that economic assistance is merely repayment for past exploitation a scholarly appraisal of past history, propaganda for the masses, or merely an ill-considered outburst of irritation? How do such attitudes influence policy, if only at the level of underlying hostility and suspicions?

Though there are examples of high returns to individual firms, it is far from clear that the balance sheet for foreign enterprises in Africa would show high average profits for foreign capital. Yet it is quite widely believed that Africa has been "exploited" in the sense that excessive profits have been made. It is of interest that the United Africa Company would have been bankrupt more than once, since its formation in 1929, but for the support of Unilever. This is not to argue that Africa has or has not been exploited, but that beliefs about the past can influence attitudes and (depending on how strongly these are held) policy.

It was remarked that economists concerned with Africa are primarily interested in economic development: in descriptive and analytical aspects, or in policy considerations, or in both. The initial task is to identify specific problems. General diagnoses and prescriptions have their place in textbooks on economic development, but situations in different countries require separate studies, though of course problems may be shared by neighboring countries and countries without common frontiers may have common problems of, say, crop diseases and marketing. Empirical material is often inadequate, and it has been commonly observed how wasteful of very scarce resources inadequately prepared development plans can be. There is always room for studies of further economic development, for there are many variables, and changing circumstances mean changing production potential.

The discussion produced several other interesting, researchable possibilities for economic studies in African international relations, including (a) further evaluation of the question of whether foreign enterprises in both past and present did "exploit" African countries; (b) a study of the extent of Africa's economic importance, as a whole and by individual countries, to Europe; (c) an analysis of whether the status of association with the European Economic Community is more valuable to African states than staying outside the Community; (d) the effect of metropolitan monetary areas on intra-African and external relations; to what extent do such zones impede or advance economic growth and economic choice, economic cooperation with neighbors, the size of prospective industrial plants, and the possibilities of economies of large scale; (e) the efficiency and impact of the U.N. Economic Commission for Africa; (f) a definition and measurement of the extent of economic neocolonialism in African states; and (g) the foreign-policy implications of attempts to diversify economic dependence by expansions of trade with, and aid from, Soviet countries.

MILITARY INFLUENCES

The discussion of military influences on African foreign policies was opened by Harvey Glickman and Helen Kitchen. Since African arms and armies are weak, Glickman pointed out, military strategy per se, does not govern African foreign-policy moves. For a time, it even appeared as if African leaders were giving serious thought to attempting to eliminate military factors from intra-African relations. Not very long ago, there were suggestions for the "denuclearization" of Africa, for trying out pilot schemes of regional arms control in Africa, and for maximizing Africa's moral appeal in international affairs. Julius Nyerere once suggested that African states would not need armies for external defense as long as Pan-Africanism developed into a reality. Kenneth Kaunda has shown great interest in techniques of nonviolence and still retains ties with Quaker agencies, partially for this purpose.

For a time, Glickman remarked, it appeared that newly emergent African states might really try to carry out a "balance of feebleness" policy. In the play "Romanoff and Juliet," Peter Ustinov outlined such a policy for a small weak state in Central Europe. Weakness was seen to reward its possessor, since a weak state that was already at the mercy of others would not be a prize or worth any effort to a would-be conqueror. But the idea of such a policy rapidly diminished. African armies have now been in the field and have participated in several hostile engagements, e.g., in the Algerian-Moroccan border war and in the Ethiopian-Somalian skirmishes, as well as the extensive use of Egyptian troops outside Africa, in Yemen and against Israel.

Glickman felt, however, that the study of the role of African military forces in external security does not lead very far. Far more important is the role of the military in internal security and as a "pressure group" in the making of foreign policy. The problem of civil-military relations is the crucial area for analysis. The foreign-policy outlook of an African state depends on the character and style of its process of modernization. A "mobilization" system will tend toward a more militant policy; a "reconciliation" system will act more conservatively. *Mutatis mutandis*, civil-military relations, and hence the role of the military in foreign-policy making, hinge on the type of emergent political system.

Glickman emphasized the need to distinguish between different types of political systems. Similarities among the varieties of weakness among African states may be impressive, but the differences among them may be more important. Military coups may become most important in nonmobilization states; political struggles may take the form of a polarization of forces around the military and militant socialists.

Despite the attractions of the idea of a demilitarized Africa, African leaders have found that there are great problems in depending on diplomacy for security. Obviously, other states will not always share one's own view of interests and goals. Diplomacy also places great emphasis on negotiating skill and manipulation, which are usually products of long experience in the international arena. But the most significant pressure tending toward a "traditional" view of the need for military forces has been the dependence on international organs for problem-solving. Operations within the U.N. soon forced African states to build up national armies if they were to have any leverage in contributing to regional solutions to regional emergencies. The Congo crisis demonstrated that a foreign policy that emphasized the use of the U.N. also had to contribute to the sources of U.N. power to act.

These endemic pressures for the expansion of military forces to fulfill the attributes of nationhood, despite the absence of a primary external-security function, underlined the importance of the military in domestic affairs. For the expansion of armies means the extension of dependency relationships and the restriction of maneuverability in foreign policy. It also raises a potential internal threat to the life of a regime. Africa's experiences of successful and unsuccessful coups and mutinies lies heavily on the present-day African leadership. It must be expected, then, that African leaders will devote much time to the problem of controlling their own armies.

Armies that do not have the maintenance of external security as their primary role are bound to get drawn into domestic politics. Perhaps this is the lesson of South America, another continent of small states facing similar problems simultaneously. African leaders, aware of this, may find that the absorption of the military in the task of development may become important as a means of helping civilians to retain control.

Glickman thought that the "political" rather than the "professional" military will gain in importance. To the extent that the military must be drawn into domestic politics and the tasks of modernization, the less realistic an emphasis on professionalism becomes. As other pressure groups, such as labor, youth, women, are integrated into the process of development, it makes less sense for the military to remain isolated—at least from the point of view of the politicians. This will mean that the study of the military must be integrated with general political studies. In foreign policy, as in other areas of African life, politics remains paramount.

Helen Kitchen pointed out that in reaching any durable conclusions about the military determinants of African foreign policies, we must operate on shakier ground than in most other fields. As yet, there is only a trickle of material on the "nuts and bolts" of African military establishments, much less on the psychology and aspirations of African soldiers and officers. Opportunities for non-military persons—either African or non-African, for that matter —to get to know African military personnel on other than a superficial level are very limited. The only full-scale biography of an African military personality is Monheim's of Mobutu.

As armies become larger and technically more impressive in the race to "keep up with the Joneses," they may have a new role to play in foreign as well as domestic affairs. Mrs. Kitchen thought it necessary to be somewhat more cautious in estimating what their domestic role will be. As the revolt of the Force Publique and the 1964 mutinies in East Africa indicated, we know very little of what goes on in barracks after hours. First, by the nature of things, a disgruntled soldier does not risk court-martial prematurely by writing letters to the local press, circulating subversive pamphlets, or "sounding off" as opposition civilian politicians do. Second, a military leader may be thrust into power by events that he did not initiate—as in Lebanon—and then discover he likes it. Third, the military may find itself cooperating with another element of society, as in Dahomey and Congo (Brazzaville), without having thought through the longer-term implications of its actions. Fourth, of course, the level of force in most of Africa is so low that a very small armed group can change the destiny of a country.

Armies are, moreover, sometimes moved to drastic action by pressures that are not always comparable with those that propel civilian politicians. In Togo, the ex-servicemen who overthrew the Olympio Government in 1963 were apparently not motivated by ideological considerations but primarily by bitterness about Olympio's unwillingness to relax his austerity program and find places for them in the Togolese Army. In Egypt, middle-level army officers were deeply aware of the need for sweeping social and political reform throughout the late 1940's, but what finally moved them to begin to make serious plans to overthrow King Farouk was the ignominy of military defeat in the Palestine War. Their disquiet was fanned to open revolt by the humiliating discovery that their civilian leaders had sent them into battle with defective and inadequate arms against a stronger foe.

Mrs. Kitchen was particularly struck by the problems of recruiting an officer corps. Clearly, most African governments now believe that an essential step in decolonizing armies is to broaden their base and ensure against the formation of tribal units. The Guinean Army and the new Tanzanian Army are examples of more drastic efforts to create tribally mixed, politically indoctrinated "people's armies." The political reasons are obvious: the army's self-image must be changed from that of an elite, privileged group concerned with suppression to that of a servant of all the people and of the government.

It is obviously easier to find enlisted men than officers for this kind of an army. For even when every political precaution is taken against creation of an elitist cult, the military officer, if he is good in his profession, does have a different set of values and a different approach to discipline than his civilian peers.

The armies in Africa with greatest élan and professional pride are those whose members have fought wars—e.g., those of Sudan, Senegal, Upper Volta, Egypt, Morocco, Algeria. The Egyptian Army was a poor excuse for an army until after the Palestine War. Sékou Touré has said that the participation of Guinean units in the U.N. military operation in the Congo was a major factor in forging "a new military tradition." In short, armies whose functions are simply to "stand by" are inclined to lose their vigor.

Mrs. Kitchen questioned Foltz's statement that the military's "lack of political influence derives more from the strength of the political institutions than from the weakness of the military." The military was the deciding factor in the overthrow of Fulbert Youlou in Congo (Brazzaville), in the displacement of Hubert Maga in Dahomey, and in the replacement of Olympio in Togo. In none of these cases did a strong, charismatic leader appear to command authority. Some time passed before governments emerged, and none of the three countries found charismatic replacements for the former office-holders. Mrs. Kitchen suggested the need to look for additional reasons to explain why the military stayed in the background. In the Sudanese counterrevolution of November, 1964, the military moved out without resistance not because it did not have the force and not because those who wrested power had a strong leader, but rather because the military split along political lines and could no longer operate as a unified group.

In the ensuing discussion, several other participants also commented on the restraint shown by Africa's small armies in keeping out of politics. It was generally felt, however, that military intervention in politics would increase in the future.

Participants questioned the Western orientation of some of the ideas in the chapter on military determinants. One remarked that it had a Cold War bias and concentrated too much on firing power as viewed by strategists outside Africa. She felt that more attention should have been given to North Africa, since the most significant military involvements in politics and foreign policies took place in the U.A.R., Algeria, Sudan, and Ethiopia.

She also pointed out that the military organizations left behind by the colonial powers were more suspect to African nationalists than was the civil service. Consequently, the new leaders of Africa spend much time in trying to control the military—through quiet, unpublicized Africanizing and nationalizing of the military establishments.

It was also suggested that further study is needed not only of the army but of the role of the police, armed youth groups such as the *Jeunesse*, and paramilitary groups such as the Builders Brigades; their existence reflects the concern of the politicians over the need to control armies. Moreover, the role of all these military and paramilitary groups will probably increase, especially where single party states become no-party states.

Another participant thought that the present scope of Viet-Cong activities represented a challenge to Foltz's statement that modern tropical warfare is a "logistical nightmare" that requires large amounts of sophisticated equipment and spare parts. He doubted that it would take African states as long as Foltz suggested to develop their armed forces.

A speaker mentioned several increasing pressures on African military leaders to overcome their professional reluctance to assume political roles. Africanization of top military posts, for example, made personal advancement increasingly dependent on politics—often tribal politics instead of party politics. In some countries, on the other hand, the army was the one supratribal or national institution; hence the opposition in Nigeria had called for the army not only to police elections but also to conduct them. Finally, it was suggested, the emergence of a number of fledgling air forces may change the situation. The new air force elites may not exercise the same restraints that ex-colonial armies have inherited.

Cultural and Psychological Factors

Neville Dyson-Hudson and Ronald Cohen, the two discussants of Robert Lystad's chapter, suggested additional cultural factors that needed study. Dyson-Hudson thought that anthropologists could make a greater contribution than Lystad had suggested in analyzing the foreign policies of Africa's nation-states. He believed that political policies are rooted in values and might be defined as observable regularities in the pursuit of values by the political community or its representatives. He felt that rather than limiting themselves to the characteristics of small local societies on the one hand, or considering such near-continental concepts as *négritude* on the other, anthropologists could make a contribution by anchoring themselves to the national level.

As an example, he showed how the value-scheme of nomadic tribesmen in the northern Sudan determined their decision to support the Sudan against Egypt. When Egyptian troops crossed the arbitrary northern boundary of the Sudan in 1961 into the territory of the Beja tribes, the Beja felt that two of their cherished values were threatened—their tribal solidarity and influence and their nomadic way of life.

For a time, the outcome was in the balance; but it was decided by clearly considered cultural factors. The nomads of the East, like nomads elsewhere in Sudan, and of the outer regions generally, were convinced that they had been calculatedly neglected by the central government, which they saw as composed of Nile-dwellers. Their most profitable camel markets were at Aswan, in Egypt, rather than at Port Sudan, in Sudan. They contrasted their experience of Egyptian officials favorably with the reactions of their own newly incumbent countrymen. A cognate tribe (the Ababda) lived in adjacent Egyptian territory. Two clearly cultural factors finally resolved their potentially pro-Egyptian sentiments in favor of remaining in Sudan—and so threatening the Egyptian expedition with armed hostility and depredation if it remained. First, such a move would have split the Bisharin tribe of the Beja territorially, with only one of its major sections going to Egypt. There, the tribal argument ran, it would be numerically and socially inferior to, and so dependent on the whims of, the neighboring Ababda. Second, regardless of their plight in Sudan, there were far more nomads there than in Egypt, and so there was always the hope that influence might eventually be brought to bear on the central Sudanese government in their interests. In Egypt, the tribesmen contended, they would eventually be ignored even more, for only they and the Ababda would remain as unsettled nomadic groups. In the face of these two threats, the leaders of the Bisharin took a conscious, explicit, and successful stand with Sudan and against Egypt. In so doing, they decisively influenced the course of national events, for at no time was there anything but a token handful of Sudanese military to prevent a *de facto* realignment of the nation's boundaries.

Dyson-Hudson suggested that this example of cultural influence on foreign relations was not unique. As additional examples, he mentioned I. M. Lewis' research on the Somali, Audrey Richards' comments on the Baganda, and Germaine Tillion's work on Algeria. He acknowledged that such cultural influences on foreign policy have the complexity of a jigsaw puzzle, but felt that they can in fact be patiently pieced together.

Ronald Cohen also felt that anthropological study of cultural values could contribute more to the analysis of foreign policies than Lystad had indicated. Objecting to the "psychologism" of the chapter, Cohen contended that the term "cultural determinants" implied a great deal more than psychology. He proposed further research on the differing "achievement orientation" levels of indigenous cultures, to test the hypothesis that those peoples with the highest aspirations for achievement would make the greatest demands in foreign policy. He suggested that countries (e.g., Nigeria and Kenya) with well protected regional and ethnic minorities and subgroups—peoples whose cultures are constitutionally respected and safeguarded—compromise more often in foreign-policy disputes than those new countries (e.g., Ghana and Guinea) whose ethnic groups are not protected and where there is a political culture of uncompromising insistence on loyalty to stipulated national goals.

Finally, Cohen suggested that it is a challenge to anthropology to give more attention to the "new cultures" that are emerging among the elites of Africa; new questions must be asked regarding education, urbanism (as opposed to urbanization), literature, mass media, and the nature and level of participation in national life. The answers to those questions would provide the basis for additional evaluation of cultural influences on African foreign policies.

In the ensuing discussion, several participants questioned Lystad's emphasis on "hostility" and "aggressiveness" as psychocultural traits resulting from the acculturation process in the rapidly changing societies of Africa. One of the Africans present suggested that these traits are no more present in Africa than in the United States and that they are universal in the sense that they characterize certain individuals in all societies. Lystad agreed that the traits were universal but felt that they are generally more intense in transitional societies. A great deal of research in this field has been undertaken but little of it has thus far been done in Africa. It would therefore be useful to undertake African case studies to test the hypothesis that the acculturation process in rapidly changing transitional societies is a psychocultural experience that tends to breed hostility and aggressiveness.

These questions raised the idea of "national character" studies, and stimulated debate over the role of anthropology in foreign-policy research. What is there that is peculiarly "African" in African foreign policies, and what light can anthropology, with its traditional focus on small groups and limited subjects, throw on the behavior of national societies? Mali was mentioned as an example of a state where national pride had historic roots.

A participant proposed an investigation of traditional African characteristics of "verbal violence," such as the use of shrill exhortations, accusations, slogans, and vindictives. When these appear in the press or in the public utterances of politicians, they are often interpreted by foreign journalists and diplomats as the point of view of the government, especially where one-party systems control the media of communication. A newspaper headline in Ghana, for example, proclaimed: BRITAIN MURDERS HAMMARSKJOLD. A cultural analysis of such verbal behavior could be made to uncover language styles in the vernacular which might be guiding the speaker or writer in his choice of words in English or French. The differing attitudes of Africans toward each other's verbal violence should also be studied. For example, the startled Somalis declared *persona non grata* a Ghanaian ambassador to Somalia who denounced an American journalist as "this pink, cancerous, leperous neocolonialist of a woman" because she had publicized a strain in Ghana-Somalia relations.

A second dimension of a study of verbal violence could appraise how many or how few people in a given country are influenced by such exhortations in their own mass media. For example, did even Convention People's Party stalwarts take the slogans of the Ghanaian press seriously? Isn't the main effect of the press to irritate outsiders? Isn't it counterproductive for Westerners to react by freezing AID programs at present levels and by demanding apologies? Aren't the most vital impressions received by Africans those that are transmitted orally rather than in the press?

Such a study might also compare the habits of both adults and children in the use of verbal violence as opposed to physical violence. Ga fishermen in Ghana reach crescendos of verbal violence in arguing over the catch in a net, without striking a physical blow. Would it be found that today's Ghanaians are largely pacifists in reconciling disputes?

The relationship between hostility and intimacy might also be a worthy object of study. One could test the hypothesis that kinship-oriented societies tend to use sharp talk with intimates and formal discourse with strangers. This is even true, it was suggested, among developed peoples; for example, French protestations and criticisms of Americans have something of the quality of a family quarrel in contrast to the formalism with which the French deal with the Russians and Chinese. To Americans, the French often appear more friendly to the Russians and Chinese when, in fact, the opposite is true. Possibly the same thing is true of kinship-minded Africans who feel they can take greater verbal liberties with their former masters or their cousins (Americans) than with the exotic people from the Urals or from the landmass of Asia.

It was also suggested that there is a need for better understanding of African traditional gift behavior in so far as it has significance for diplomacy and foreign aid. How can donors of foreign aid help the recipient maintain his self-esteem by practicing reciprocity? Ben Bella's gift of money to the Kennedy library, Nasser's gift of a Nile temple to Washington, Haile Selassie's establishment of prizes for research on Africa and on Ethiopia, and African offers of scholarships to Americans were mentioned as examples of African reciprocity to redress the balance and to psychologically relieve African feelings of dependence (and therefore hostility) toward foreign benefactors. We need to study our own cultural aversion to receiving gifts from others, learn to dissociate such behavior from bribes, and learn to put "better chosen" strings on our aid.

POLITICAL DETERMINANTS

Douglas Anglin and Nathan Shamuyarira were the discussants of Gray Cowan's chapter on domestic and intra-African determinants of African foreign policies. Anglin stressed the importance of the domestic political determinants inside each state. He felt that more attention should be given to the effects of the colonial experience in determining Africans' attitudes not only toward their former metropoles but toward international relations generally. Particularly important, he said, is the manner in which independence was attained. Leaders of the many states that obtained independence without violence seemed to think that a similar process might work in the white redoubt in Southern Africa, while Algeria, which had to fight for its freedom, had a very different approach toward solving the Rhodesian problem, for example.

A second domestic political determinant is the way in which the nature of domestic institutions affected attitudes toward other countries. Nigeria's federalism and Ghana's rejection of federalism at home conditioned their respective attitudes toward federalism for the Congo, Central Africa, East Africa, and Pan-Africa.

Anglin and several other participants noted that foreign policy is often a projection of *party* politics. Current Nigerian attitudes toward Arabs and Israelis stem from arguments the Action Group utilized before the Minorities Commission in 1957 to support its demand for a Middle Belt State. Similarly, Northern Peoples' Congress attacks on Israeli policy were a means of attacking the Western Region Government. In Kenya as well, intraparty struggles for power often take the form of arguments over foreign policy.

The degree of national unity within a state is a fourth factor affecting foreign policy. International and especially intra-African relations are conducted on the same basis as intergroup relations internally: highly centralized states such as Ghana lack experience in techniques of cooperation and compromise necessary in deal-ings with neighbors and others, while deeply divided states like the Congo are so preoccupied with internal affairs as to be unable to play an effective role externally.

Finally, the operative ideologies of domestic ruling groups often have counterparts in foreign policy. Radicalism at home breeds radicalism abroad, though, as in the case of Uganda, radicalism in foreign policy is in part a substitute for an inability to implement radicalism at home. Morocco, in a different way, is also an excep-tion to the rule.

The belief in the need for ideological justification for domestic and foreign policies is so strong that even pragmatism is elevated into an ideology. The rejection of "extreme capitalism" and "crude Communism" requires ideological justification. This is the real significance of African socialism. The foreign-policy implica-tions of African socialism merit more attention than they have thus far received. Two ideas are involved here: first, nonalign-ment, or the rejection of European ideologies in favor of some-thing thought to be African, and second, African solidarity, which is explained as an extension of "Harambee" or the tradi-tional spirit of cooperation. Whether or not this is a correct inter-pretation of African traditions is less important than that the myth is being created.

In conclusion, Anglin suggested that if foreign policy is largely a projection of domestic policies or politics, obviously the study of African foreign policies requires a much greater understanding of domestic determinants than we now possess.

Noting the many references in various chapters to the African states' heavy dependence on their former European metropoles for financial and military aid, Nathan Shamuyarira stated that greater stress should be placed on the keenness of African leaders to bring an end to "paper" independence. African desires for greater economic independence have led to a continued drive for collective security through the OAU, and for multilateral aid through the United Nations, specifically through ECA and UNTA.

Shamuyarira felt that, in their treatment of nonalignment, the authors of certain chapters should have further emphasized that many African leaders choose nonalignment in a positive desire to act as a "ball bearing" between Communist and Western powers, thereby reducing friction and contributing to world peace. Such leaders feel that if they join either power group they lose their ability to influence the other big powers.

Criticizing Cowan's reference to the uninformed nature of mass publics in Africa, Shamuyarira cited Gabriel Almond to support his contention that the masses throughout the world generally are uninformed on foreign-policy issues and that foreign policy is mainly of interest to specific pressure groups. In the ensuing discussion, other speakers emphasized the role of pressure groups in Africa as a topic that could benefit from further analysis. In a related point, Shamuyarira suggested that more study should be given to the role of political parties in shaping foreign policy. The stronger the political party, the greater its pressures on the leader. Moreover, the leader is able to be far more forceful if he has the backing of a strong party.

Shamuyarira stated an additional reason for eliminating the white redoubt in South and Southern Africa: As long as a million whites can look over their shoulders to South Africa, they will not settle securely inside African states, and they will become a source of tension, insecurity, danger, and even possible subversion from South Africa. Already, Shamuyarira said, South African planes are flying over some African countries to do high-altitude photography.

Shamuyarira objected to the categorization of African states as "radical" and "moderate" or "revolutionary" and "nonrevolutionary." Such categorization might be useful in the United States, but it causes confusion and conflict in Africa. An African leader may be embarrassed to know that he is now regarded as a "moderate" or as one who stands for the *status quo*. Categories should be less rigid than those used in most of the papers.

Shamuyarira also suggested that Cowan overemphasized the differences between the states that are committed to the African revolution and those that are not. We must define what is meant by "the African revolution." If the term means cutting the economic apron strings of Europe and achieving continental unity—despite all the difficulties of communication, ethnic differences, language, and religion—research may show fewer differences than implied. The so-called Casablanca and Monrovia groups appear to have differed on method or approach to unity—political or economic integration—and not so much on commitment to those ideals. Shamuyarira recognized, however, that some states have made more noise than others.

Agreeing that terms such as "radical" and "moderate" are unsatisfactory, some participants suggested a variety of substitutes, but tended to use those labels nonetheless. The research need presented itself in several ways: What categories are really relevant? What are the criteria for establishing categories? What is unique and what is universal in African political ideas?

A participant noted that Canada's "paper independence" had not prevented its economic development. Independence was less a status than a habit of mind and action. "To be independent was to act independently." Another participant suggested that this question was related to the psychocultural factors discussed in Lystad's chapter, and was worthy of further study. He also saw a possible link between Lystad's hostility syndrome and the quest for full independence leading to the extension of the revolution through subversion. If there is a distinction between radicals and moderates, it may be the difference between those who believe that to be independent is to *act* independently, even if the action is counterproductive, and those who believe that independence consists of being able to *decide* independently, e.g., to decide whether or not to maintain bilateral relations with the former metropole.

Another speaker noted a good deal of mythology in the cultural aspects of "African socialism." In particular, he considered African family solidarity to be a myth, since he had found in Bornu that 93 per cent of marriages ended in divorce. He also found a good deal of myth in the belief that African property holding is communal in nature; to be a leader, one must have the right to transfer land. Shamuyarira responded that, irrespective of divorce and land transfer, African solidarity is a reality; it means that there are no African millionaires and that Africans can come for help to their kinsmen as of right, not of privilege.

Several participants raised questions for study about the effect of counterproductive actions by Presidents Nasser and Nkrumah on their respective foreign policies. What happens when the leaders feel the revolution is failing? What effect has their recent "isolation" had on the foreign policies of the radical leaders? And how will the waning influence of Nasser and Nkrumah affect the activities of other African leaders? What will be the effect on the radical leaders if their followers lose faith in the ability of the revolution to satisfy their expectations? Will the leaders compromise or become more extreme?

According to Gray Cowan, the radicals are learning that they must not separate themselves from other leaders so far that they lose all influence. Cowan and other speakers felt, however, that Nkrumah's influence was *not* on the wane, especially among the younger generation of Africans who were drawn to him as a "militant or forceful or dynamic" leader, and who did not respond to "weak or soft or conciliatory" personalities. Another aspect of Ghana's influence was also noted—its unilateral action in interstate dealings. Though not a member of the Organization of African Unity's Liberation Committee, Ghana provided unilateral aid to independence movements, a step which possibly gave Ghana greater influence in Southern Africa than if it had acted through the Committee.

An African participant felt that not enough attention had been paid to the traditional leaders, particularly in countries where no drastic action had been undertaken to lessen the powers of paramount chiefs. He thought that after the first flush of independence is over, after new types of leaders have arisen, the African people may turn again to those leaders with whom they were traditionally more familiar.

Crawford Young, one of the discussants at a final session, emphasized the need for elite socialization research studies of the makers of African foreign policies. Who are the foreign-policy decision-makers, how did they attain their roles, and what are their general characteristics? Although another speaker noted that biographical data alone could not meaningfully explain decisions, there was general agreement that a great deal more must be known about the foreign-policy decision-makers. Since they form only a small percentage of the population, and the elites of various countries have both shared and distinguishing characteristics, comparative elite research would be desirable and feasible. Criteria to be examined might include age, level, and type of education, travel (especially abroad), family background under the colonial system, impact of the colonial system on the type of elite being studied, economic interests, religious interests, role in the independence struggle, role in the postindependence period, and the characteristics and perceptions that are held and shared by occupants of different types of role positions. The need for further study of traditional leaders and their possible future roles was also emphasized.

EXTERNAL POLITICAL PRESSURES

The discussion of the influence of external pressures as a determinant of African foreign policies was opened by John Karefa-Smart and William H. Lewis. Dr. Karefa-Smart added four points to C. T. Thorne's comprehensive chapter on the subject. First, he pointed out that the very notion of "foreign policy" is of secondary importance in Africa; it is significant primarily in connection with the necessity of U.N. membership, and in the receiving and sending of diplomatic missions as an external evidence of independence and national sovereignty. Ministries of Foreign Affairs are a colonial heritage, and in African countries the Foreign Minister does not necessarily rank next to the Prime Minister in the order of protocol.

The most important attempts to involve African states in world affairs come from the Arab states of North Africa. Karefa-Smart remarked that he considered this an obstacle to Pan-African unity because those states gave priority to "Arabness" rather than to "Africanness." The Arab presence in Africa, he added, was a relic of colonialism comparable to European colonialism, and there is "no real conviction that we belong together."

In the third place, he felt that more emphasis should be placed on the effect of race relations in the United States on African thinking. The racial situation in the United States evokes an attitude of mind among African leaders that influences their response to any U.S. diplomatic gestures.

Finally, Karefa-Smart commented on the effort by the United Kingdom to retain political influence in its former territories by insisting on retaining the position of the British Queen not only as "Head of the Commonwealth" but also as Monarch. This is politically significant because it limits the extent to which an African country with an expatriate British Queen can really be nonaligned in foreign policy. In the Sierra Leone Constitution, the clause that says Parliament consists of the Queen and the Houses of Parliament is an entrenched clause that requires a two-thirds majority, followed by approval by the voters, for repeal. The latter requirement helps to entrench it further because politicians don't like to have to "go to the country."

William H. Lewis contributed several suggestions for research on African international relations: (1) *Political kinetics*—emphasis upon categories of African reactions to various types of stimuli. Lewis pointed out that, like most other world leaders, African leaders tend to become more deeply involved in reacting to such tangible "threats" as intervention, aggression, and subversion. However, little comparative research has been conducted on the threshold of responses and intensities of sentiment under conditions of indirect, as opposed to direct, "threats." (2) *Decision-making processes* in formulating and executing foreign policies also require research in depth. Western scholars require a more profound appreciation of the personalized nature of these processes, as compared with the generally institutionalized pattern encountered in the United States. (3) *Situation analysis* also will aid in gaining an appreciation of the nonintegrated aspects of policy-making. (4) More structure and rigor also are required in treating with *strategies, forces, objectives, "reciprocal expectations,"* and rules of conduct.

The actual process by which decisions are made also was singled out by several other participants as a subject for further study. Not only is the mechanics of decision-making in African countries different from that in developed states, but it varies from one African country to another. The Foreign Ministry may play a considerable role in one country, while the personal political advisers of the head of state may play a decisive role in another. What is the role of the central bank, the military, the police? To what extent do international agencies set limits to the options available to the leaders? Do opposition groups limit the options of the group in power? And to what extent do decisions taken by other states determine the foreign-policy reactions and decisions of African leaders?

Situational studies—detailed case studies of how African states have reacted to concrete foreign-policy situations—would help to answer some of these questions. Participants also called attention to the need for comprehensive country studies of individual states as a necessary basis for analysis of foreign policy. In addition, several speakers suggested the need for comparative studies not only among African countries but with other world areas. Examples given included the OAU and the OAS, Pan-Arabism and Pan-Africanism, Asian solidarity efforts after 1945 and African solidarity efforts after 1960.

In the discussion that followed, attention was called to the need for study of "leverage through weakness," or the "balance of feebleness," or "weakness as a source of strength" in the new states. The nature of African dependence and the exact character of its effect on foreign policy needs further clarification. It could illuminate how the weak states of Africa are able to exercise influence beyond their material means by drawing in outside powers, forcing them to involve themselves, and by threatening disorder and collapse.

The foreign-policy implications of having "vassal states" that lack even minimal resources was mentioned. One speaker remarked that Congo (Brazzaville) could be considered a vassal state whose vulnerability to Chinese influence has been made possible by French withdrawal—a situation that may be duplicated dangerously in other small states in the French sphere of influence if France withdraws further. Malawi may become subject to the same Cold War pressures if President Banda's control is ended. It was suggested that U.S. foreign-policy makers should be taking much more cognizance of these danger areas, or potential danger areas, particularly those close to the Congo or to the white redoubt.

A participant commented that Thorne tended to corroborate some of the theses set forth in other chapters such as (a) the "frustration" in the Congo peace-keeping operation, which, despite efforts to Africanize it, depended to a great extent on the logistical support of non-African states and (b) on leverage through weakness. He concluded by suggesting that it was remarkable that African states can develop foreign policies at all in view of the fact that they must spend most of their time in merely reacting to day-to-day pressures.

On the question of Afro-Asian solidarity, it was suggested that in the future there would probably be a tendency in the U.N. for each state to act more independently in relation to its own national interests. More study is needed on the question of how effective the Chinese really are in their utilization of racial factors, particularly in their identification of themselves as "nonwhites."

The involvement of the United States in colonial and neo-colonial situations was referred to by several participants. One of them asked why the United States continues to pretend that it was not a party to the partition of Africa in the late nineteenth century. Another remarked that the United States is getting more and more into a colonialist and neocolonialist posture by its activities in Viet-Nam, the Dominican Republic, and the Congo. African suspicions of American neocolonialism were fostered by CIA activities as well as by those observers who seem pleased by the split within the Organization of African Unity.

Another speaker recalled the research of the British historians Ronald Robinson and John Gallagher, who challenged the old view that the early and mid-nineteenth century was an anti-imperialist interlude in British policy, and stressed instead the "fundamental continuity" in British expansion throughout the nineteenth century. The needs of British strategy and commerce were met by a variety of techniques varying from the "informal empire" of free trade, when possible, to the "formal empire" of annexation when necessary. Research along these lines could test whether Britain's decolonization since World War II could be considered a return to the technique of informal empire; and, if so, to what extent could it be considered neocolonialist? The question was also asked whether the containment policy of the United States is gradually, if unwittingly, leading it into propping up an informal empire of neocolonialist political outposts around the world.

Thorne's statement that Africa has "caught the sympathy of the developed world" was questioned by a participant who thought this feeling had greatly diminished since the Congo crisis. He wondered whether African leaders were taking into account the fact that, in their plans, they might no longer be able to count on the sympathies of the industrialized nations. He also doubted Thorne's view that in the outside world there is "an appreciation of the odds against which African leaders struggle."

Further consideration should be given to the role of the intellectual and scientific communities in Africa's international relations, taking into special account Africa's insistence on nonalignment. A participant thought that African universities have a greater chance than universities in the United States, the U.S.S.R., or China to become "intellectual free trade zones." Africans are literally more universal in their approach to the whole world than universities in the Western or Communist blocs. American professors have a better chance to meet ideologically forbidden counterparts from countries the United States does not recognize by joining an African faculty than by staying home. The same is true for Chinese, Cubans, or others coming to Africa.

Scientific and technical knowledge is vital to the modernization process. Nonalignment permits freer exposure to science and technology from all quarters except South Africa, whose *apartheid* policy prevents it from making the scientific and technical contributions it could be making to the rest of Africa. International scientific organizations provide a palatable, apolitical network within which Africans can give and receive. These organizations deserve study as a new form of both international and intra-African cooperation and association, cutting across ideological lines as well as internal African groupings.

The many forms of interaction between internal and international forces was one of the most widely recurring themes of discussion. For example, biographical research on the interpersonal relations of African leaders from various countries both before and after independence would be useful. It would also be illuminating to study the way in which the Communist Chinese, an external force, managed to penetrate and interact effectively with an internal force that had historical continuity and a traditional role in seeking power in Brazzaville. In Burundi, also, the Chinese "plugged into an established elect." A key point for study, an African participant suggested, was the activity of the Chinese Embassy in Paris, since the Africans who would rule in the French-speaking countries of Africa in 1980 were now studying in Paris.

Another participant called attention to four internal factors that need further study because of their effects on foreign policy: (1) The African attitude expressed in the phrase "We dislike this foreign country's policies, but we trust the *people* who expound and administer them." Analysis of the reasoning behind continued membership in the Commonwealth, and of popular feeling for British royalty and traditional British symbols and traditions could be instructive. Such an inquiry could also apply to the African image of Communism. Its application to Moscow and Peking might be: "We like your ideas but we don't like your methods, and we're not sure that we trust your representatives." (2) Differences in political style as indicated, for example, in the different methods used by Nyerere and Nkrumah in giving legal or constitutional effect to one-party government. (3) The African conception of the role of a political opposition. This is obviously different from the Western conception, but careful analysis could be designed to show how it is different and why. In Ghana, vigorous criticism of Nkrumah was combined with the belief by some sophisticated opponents that he should remain in power. (4) The significance of constitutionalism in Africa. Of the nine former British colonies, only two—Ghana and Tanzania—do *not* have entrenched Bills of Rights. The remainder have systems of government that include machinery for the enforcement of fundamental freedoms modeled on the Universal Declaration and the Rome Convention of 1950. Why, when they became independent, seven states chose to accept restraints on the political power of the majority, and why—so far, anyhow—they continue to recognize them and—to a greater or lesser extent—apply them in practice, are questions whose pursuit could be fruitful. Although it is concerned essentially with structural questions—i.e., institutions and procedures, which are usually subordinate to underlying political pressures—a constitution itself *can* be a political force. If the constitutional lawyer tends to attach too much importance to the significance of constitutional structure, perhaps the political scientist fails to pay enough attention to the part that a constitution can play in influencing political processes.

Howard Wriggins, a discussant at a final session on research subjects, methods, and approaches, called attention to a number of opportunities for policy-oriented research. The policy-maker is confronted by the problem of finding reliable generalizations from the past to apply to unprecedented present situations for the purpose of predicting the future. The scholar does not publish until he is certain, but the policy-maker must avoid "the paralysis of analysis." Wriggins felt, however, that the alleged "value neutrality" of the scholar as opposed to the policy-maker's alleged commitment to the national interest was overdrawn; both parties, he thought, are situated somewhere between these two characterizations. He felt that many fascinating and urgent policy problems require as much rigor as scholarly problems. As an example, he mentioned the problem of analyzing what the consequences would be if the level of foreign aid to Africa diminishes. He also questioned whether the bulk of U.S. decisions and actions regarding Africa, taken as a whole, really have much impact on that continent.

Another speaker called attention to the utility of research itself as a possible determinant of African foreign policies. Ideally, if research took full advantage of the contributions of African scholars, it should not only cast light upon the foreign policy decision-making process in African countries, but the results should lead, as well, to an improvement in the quality of the decisions. Economic, political, military, and ideological concepts such as national independence are very important to African decision-makers. But can't we design some research projects that will cast clearer light on economic alternatives and possibilities for Africa, and others that will improve understanding of the limitations on sovereignty which nations confront in the increasingly interdependent world of today?

RESEARCH BY AFRICANS

Since *African Diplomacy* deals with contemporary politics, it may arouse political sensitivities in African circles. The authors nonetheless hope that it will stimulate additional research on the foreign relations and foreign policies of African states—a subject of growing importance for both Africa and the outside world. It would be particularly valuable to have more analyses by African scholars written from African points of view. American scholars warmly applaud these words of Kenneth Onwuka Dike, distinguished Nigerian historian: "We Africans feel the time has now come for us to speak for ourselves and to take to ourselves the obligation to study with thoroughness and depth our own past and our own present and our own prospects."

After reading the symposium papers and listening to some of the discussion, one of the African participants remarked humorously that he had the weird sensation of being operated on without an anesthetic. Americans responded with the hope that African scholars might bring their perspectives to bear in dissecting the outside world. They might, for example, undertake a comparison of Gaullism with the "cargo cults" of the South Pacific, or a behavioral analysis of the "radical right" in the American Presidential election of 1964!

These whimsical exchanges reflected a growing concern in the American academic community over African reactions to the activities of American scholars in Africa today. Part of the problem arises from the wealth and size and character of the United States, a country with more than 2,000 higher educational institutions. America's pluralistic society has a high degree of uncoordinated individual initiative; and in the last decade, there has been a large and rapid increase in the number of scholars and graduate students devoting themselves to African studies. The resulting "inundation" of Africa by American researchers, and the practical problems it creates, was the subject of careful consideration at the eighth annual meeting of the African Studies Association at Philadelphia in October, 1965. Like all scholars, these Americans are curious, or they would not be scholars in the first place, and their curiosity is sometimes disturbing. Not surprisingly, Africans occasionally ask whether they are agents of the United States Government. Anthropologists are sometimes accused of trying to publicize only the most backward aspects of Africa, and political scientists are criticized for intervening in contemporary African political affairs.

It is true that in recent years American universities and foundations often have justified their efforts to develop African studies on the grounds of national interest. Increasingly, moreover, American universities (like those of every other country in the world) are accepting government funds to help meet the financial burdens of teaching and research. It is also true that many leading Africanists in the United States have served as consultants to the Department of State, the Agency for International Development, and other government bodies; and they have participated in training programs for present and future government employees. This does not make them agents of the U.S. Government, however. It is a reflection of the government's growing recognition, since the mid-1930's, of the resources that the academic community can bring to bear on problems of public policy.

The Africanists of the United States believe that American foreign-policy makers need the best advice they can get from specialists on Africa both inside and outside government. At the same time, they are acutely aware of the danger to independent judgment that arises when scholars are linked too closely with any public institution or with any given government policy. In the American tradition, this awareness extends far beyond the relatively narrow field of African studies to all aspects of the relationship between government and academic life. In fact, many Americans begin with the premise that government is probably not right about anything. And many Africanists are highly critical of U.S. policies toward Africa.

The independence of the academic community is a valued aspect of the American tradition. It brings much unsolicited advice to the government and stimulates government to seek advice. A good example of the latter was the action of Assistant Secretary of State G. Mennen Williams in creating a new Advisory Council on African Affairs in June, 1962. Composed of about forty specialists on Africa, about half of them from the academic world, the Council performs a valuable service by confronting governmental officials with African and Africanist views. Although their detached judgments and recommendations may not be accepted, the academics nonetheless stimulate officials to rethink their policies and benefit both Africa and the United States in the long run.

Scholars the world over have a common bond in the search for truth, and they need to understand one another's perspectives in order to attain it. That is why American scholars hope for the continued growth of cooperation with African scholars in both individual and team efforts. As Africa's many new universities grow, creative opportunities for fruitful cooperation in both teaching and research will multiply.

The turbulent politics of this transition period has a natural tendency to jeopardize scholarship. It is therefore all the more important for scholars to hold fast to the ideal of rigorous objectivity. The highest standard of objectivity, however, does not deny the right of scholars to different points of view. It recognizes the existence of divergent preconceptions in varying climates of opinion. As the historian Carl Becker concluded, the most objective man is the one who is most fully aware of his own preconceptions and who takes them into fullest account in formulating his judgments.